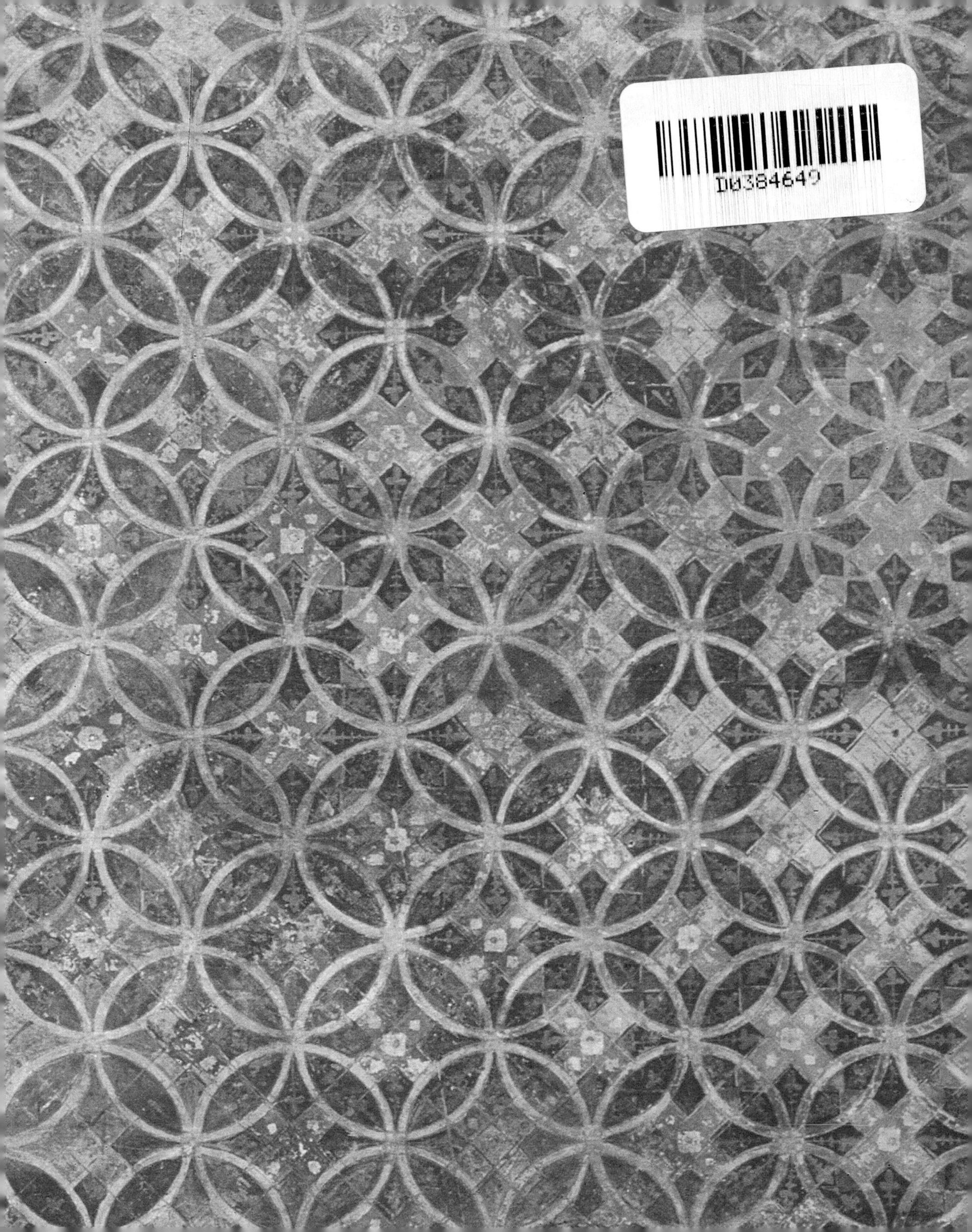
D0384649

PENGUIN STUDIO
Published by the Penguin Group
Penguin Putnam Inc., 375 Hudson Street, New York, New York 10014, U.S.A.
Penguin Books Ltd, 27 Wrights Lane, London W8 5TZ, England
Penguin Books Australia Ltd, Ringwood, Victoria, Australia
Penguin Books Canada Ltd, 10 Alcorn Avenue, Toronto, Ontario, Canada M4V 3B2
Penguin Books (N.Z.) Ltd, 182-190 Wairau Road, Auckland 10, New Zealand
Penguin India, 210 Chiranjiv Tower, 43 Nehru Place, New Delhi 11009, India

Penguin Books Ltd, Registered Offices:
Harmondsworth, Middlesex, England

First American edition
Published in 1999 by Penguin Studio,
a member of Penguin Putnam Inc.

10 9 8 7 6 5 4 3 2 1

Illustrations courtesy of Scala, Florence

Grateful acknowledgment is made for permission to reprint the following material:
Extracts on pages 27, 36, and 47 reprinted with permission from the Society of St. Francis.
Extract on page 33 from *Francis: The Journey and the Dream* by Murray Bodo.
Copyright © 1988 by Murray Bodo. Used by permission of St. Anthony Messenger Press.
All rights reserved.
Other extracts from *St. Francis of Assisi, Writings and Early Biographies:*
English Omnibus of the Sources for the Life of St. Francis edited by Marion A. Habig.
Copyright © 1973 by Franciscan Herald Press.

Index of frescoes by Lynda Stephens, copyright © Frances Lincoln Limited, 1998
Introduction by Father Maximilian Mizzi OFM Conv., copyright © Frances Lincoln Limited, 1998

CIP data available

ISBN 0-670-88364-6

Set in Perpetua and Poetica Chancery IV
Printed in Italy

THE MESSAGE OF ST FRANCIS

WITH FRESCOES FROM THE BASILICA OF ST FRANCIS AT ASSISI

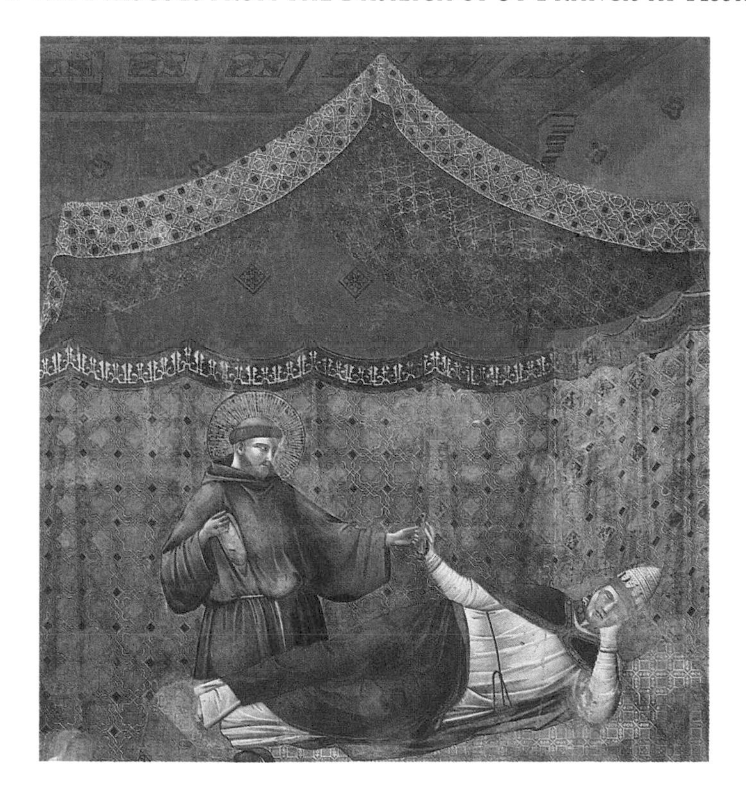

EXTRACTS SELECTED BY SISTER NAN CSF
WITH AN INTRODUCTION BY FATHER MAXIMILIAN MIZZI OFM CONV.

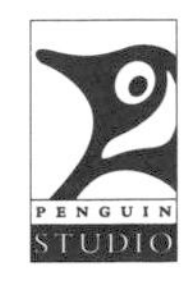

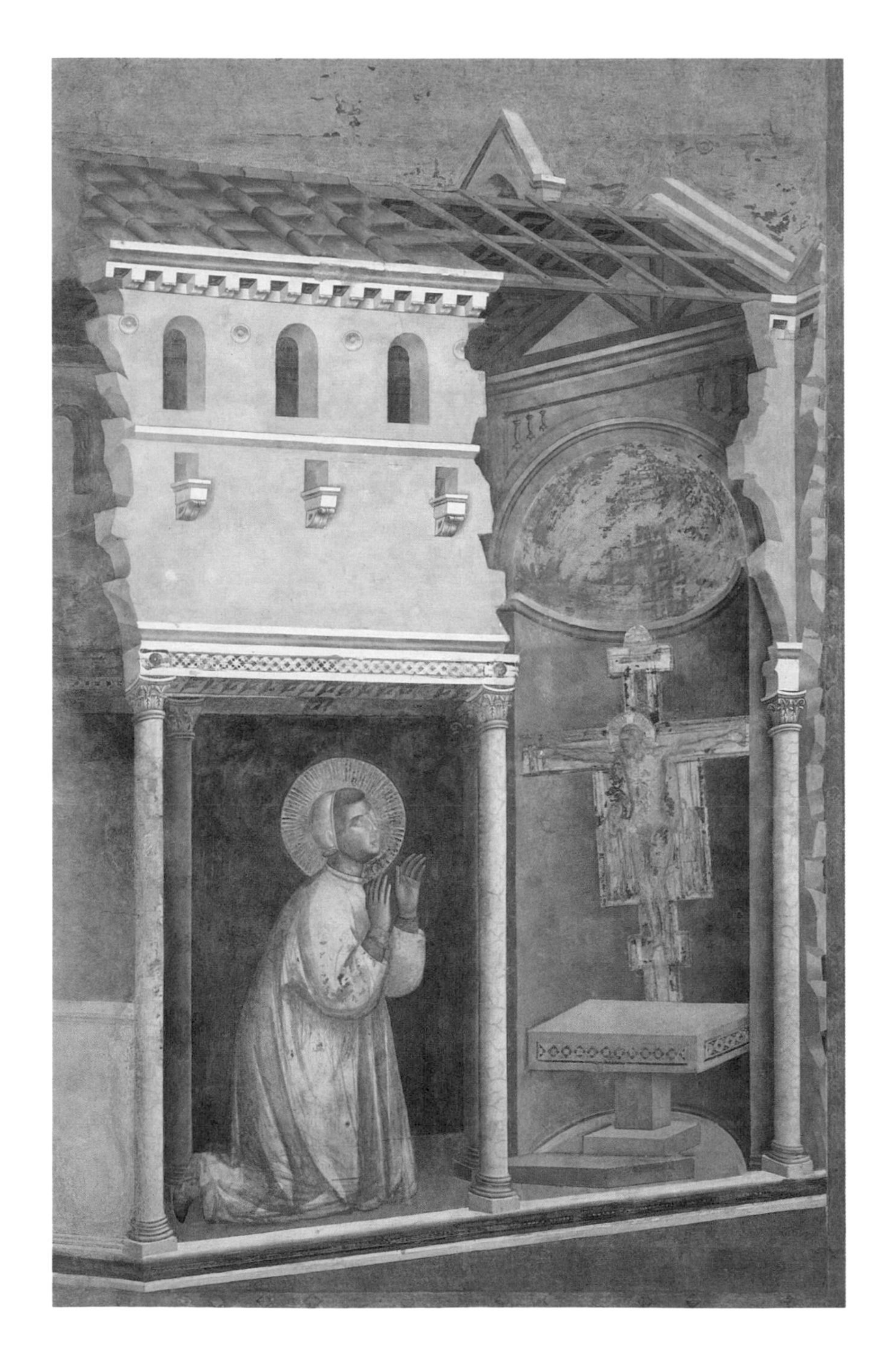

Introduction

Eight hundred years have passed since St Francis of Assisi walked through the streets in the towns and villages of Umbria, and travelled to other countries preaching the spirit of the Gospel: faith, love, poverty and joy. He praised God for the whole of creation and talked to animals about God's love. That was a long time ago. And yet his teaching and especially his lifestyle are as inspiring today as they were eight centuries ago – perhaps even more so. When Pope John Paul II visited Assisi in 1993 to pray for peace in the former Yugoslavia, he said to the friars who had gathered around him at the tomb of St Francis: "St Francis was certainly great in the thirteenth century. But we can say that he has become even more important since, and still is today."

The Basilica in Assisi enshrines both the tomb of St Francis and unique art treasures including frescoes by Cimabue, Giotto, Lorenzetti, Martini and others. The tomb makes Assisi a place of spiritual pilgrimage. Because of the frescoes depicting scenes from the Bible and from the saint's life, the Basilica is an embodiment of the message of St Francis *and* a school of art. For over seven hundred years it has kept alive the spirituality of Christ and of the saint for countless pilgrims and visitors, generation after generation.

During the last few decades, St Francis has emerged more and more as a spiritual figure second to none. The Second Vatican Council opened the way to the ecumenical movement and to an open dialogue with the world's religions. Assisi soon became the place where Christians from different churches met to pray and worship together in the spirit of St Francis.

On 27 October 1986, Pope John II invited the spiritual leaders of the main religions of the world to Assisi to pray for peace. The Franciscans welcomed them with open hearts as brothers and sisters. Assisi has thus become the city of peace and reconciliation, the city of inter-religious dialogue.

The Message of St Francis, with extracts selected by Sister Nan, a member of the Community of St Francis in London, is the right book at the right time. Illustrated with some of the most splendid frescoes from the Basilica in Assisi, it offers the reader, whether Christian or a follower of another religion, an opportunity to better discover the hidden life and teachings of St Francis. Moreover, for those seeking to deepen their spiritual life, *The Message of St Francis* offers thoughts for prayer and meditation.

Some of the precious frescoes were destroyed by the earthquake of 26 September 1997, but the spirit of St Francis remains. Perhaps Francis is called by Christ once again to repair his "church", both symbolically and literally.

Father Maximilian Mizzi OFM Conv.

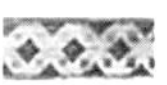

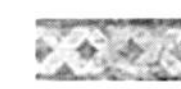

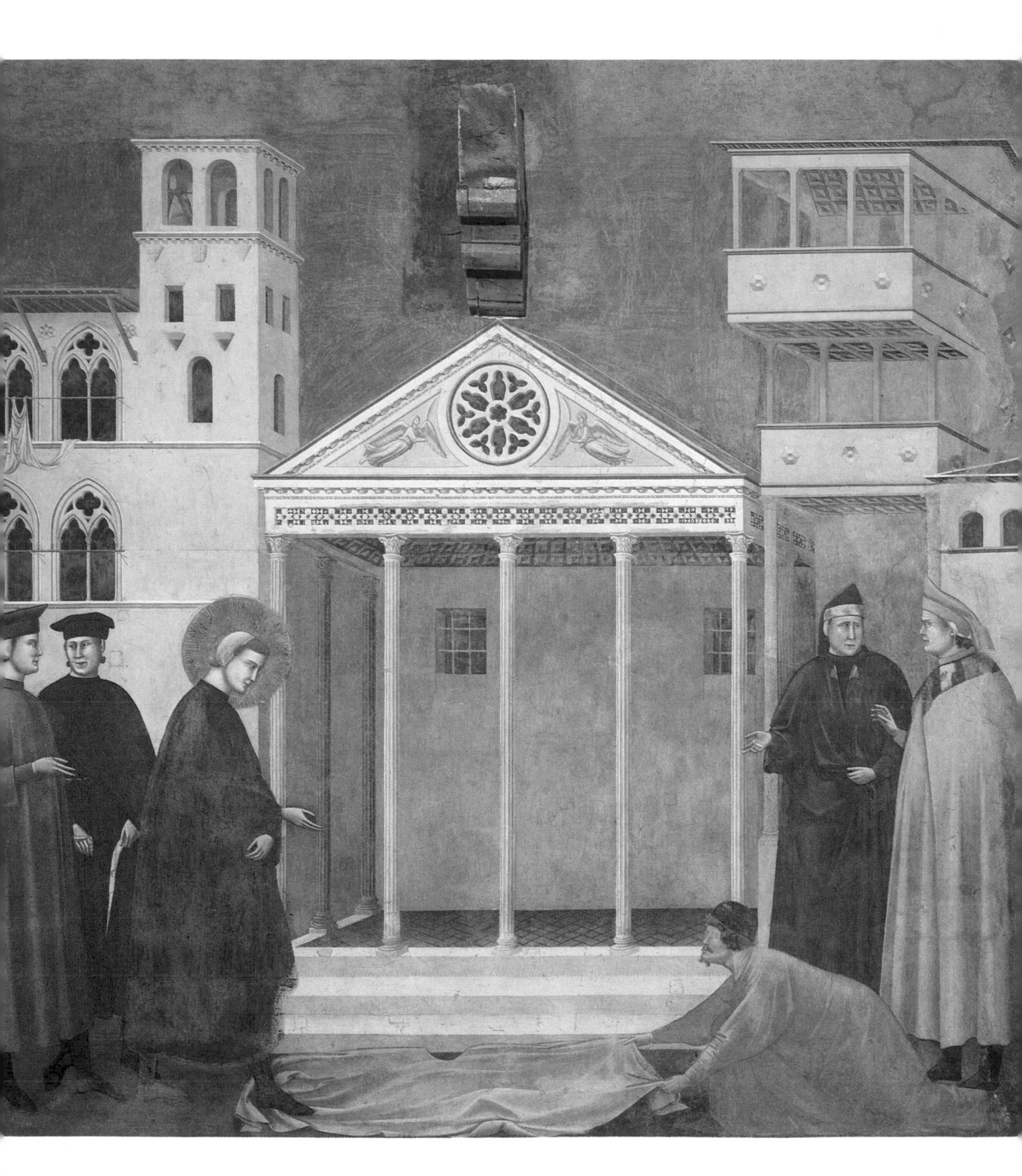

Virtue and Vice

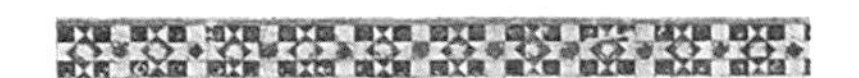

Where there is Love and Wisdom,
    there is neither Fear nor Ignorance.
Where there is Patience and Humility,
    there is neither Anger nor Annoyance.
Where there is Poverty and Joy,
    there is neither Cupidity nor Avarice.
Where there is Peace and Contemplation,
    there is neither Care nor Restlessness.
Where there is the Fear of God to guard the dwelling,
    there no enemy can enter.
Where there is Mercy and Prudence,
    there is neither Excess nor Harshness.

(*The Admonitions*, XXVII)

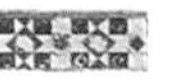

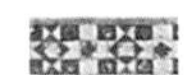

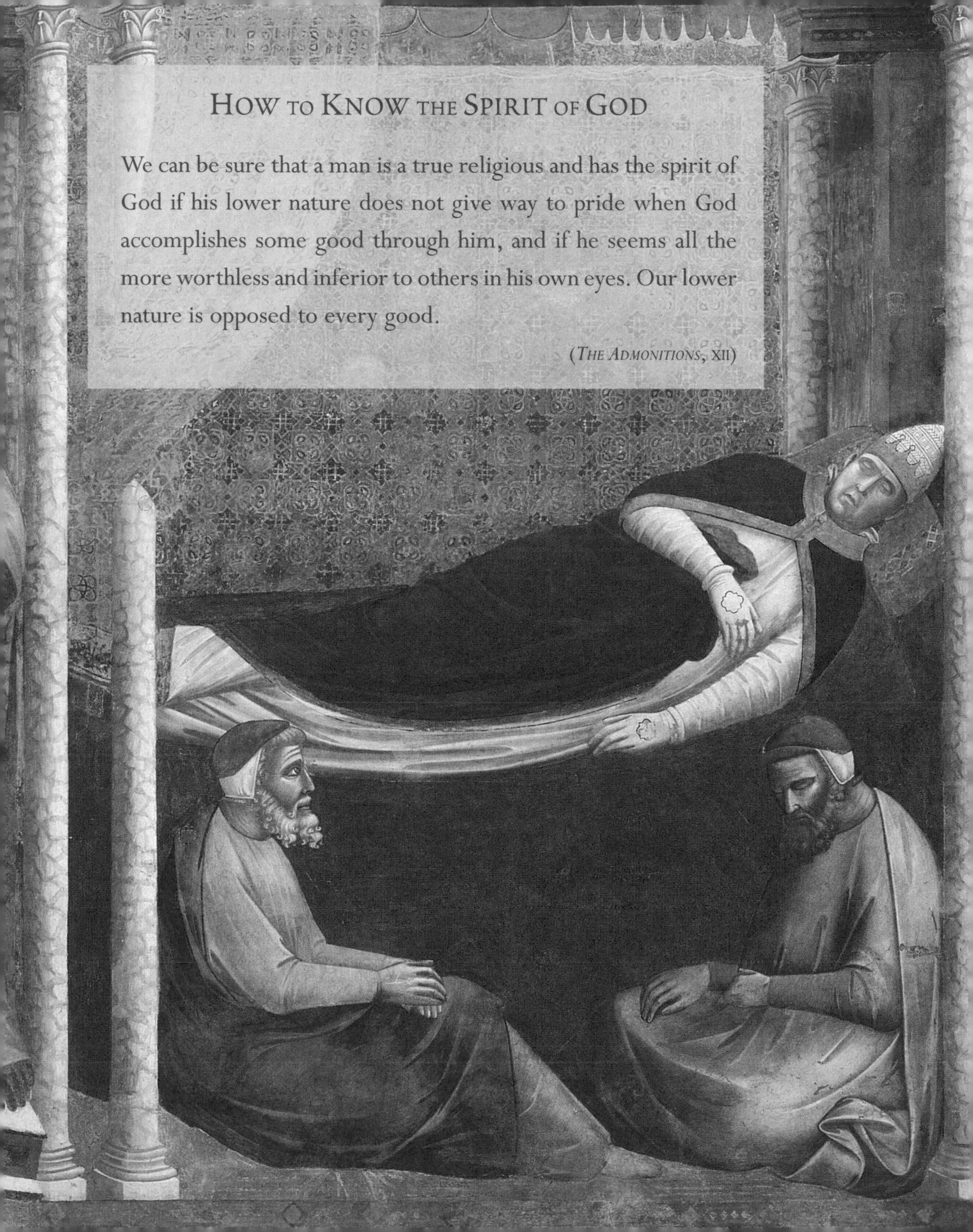

How to Know the Spirit of God

We can be sure that a man is a true religious and has the spirit of God if his lower nature does not give way to pride when God accomplishes some good through him, and if he seems all the more worthless and inferior to others in his own eyes. Our lower nature is opposed to every good.

(*The Admonitions*, XII)

Modesty is a Virtue

Blessed the religious who treasures up for heaven the favours God has given him and does not want to show them off for what he can get out of them. God himself will reveal his works to whomsoever he pleases. Blessed the religious who keeps God's marvellous doings to himself.

(*The Admonitions*, XXVIII)

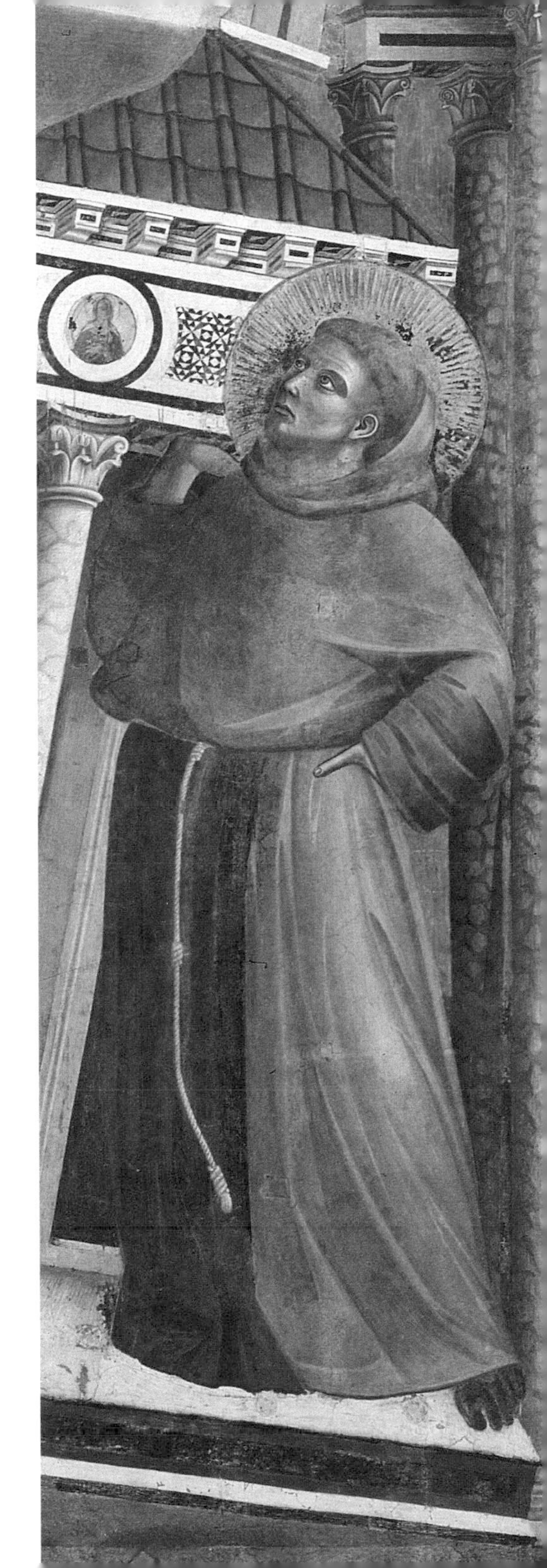

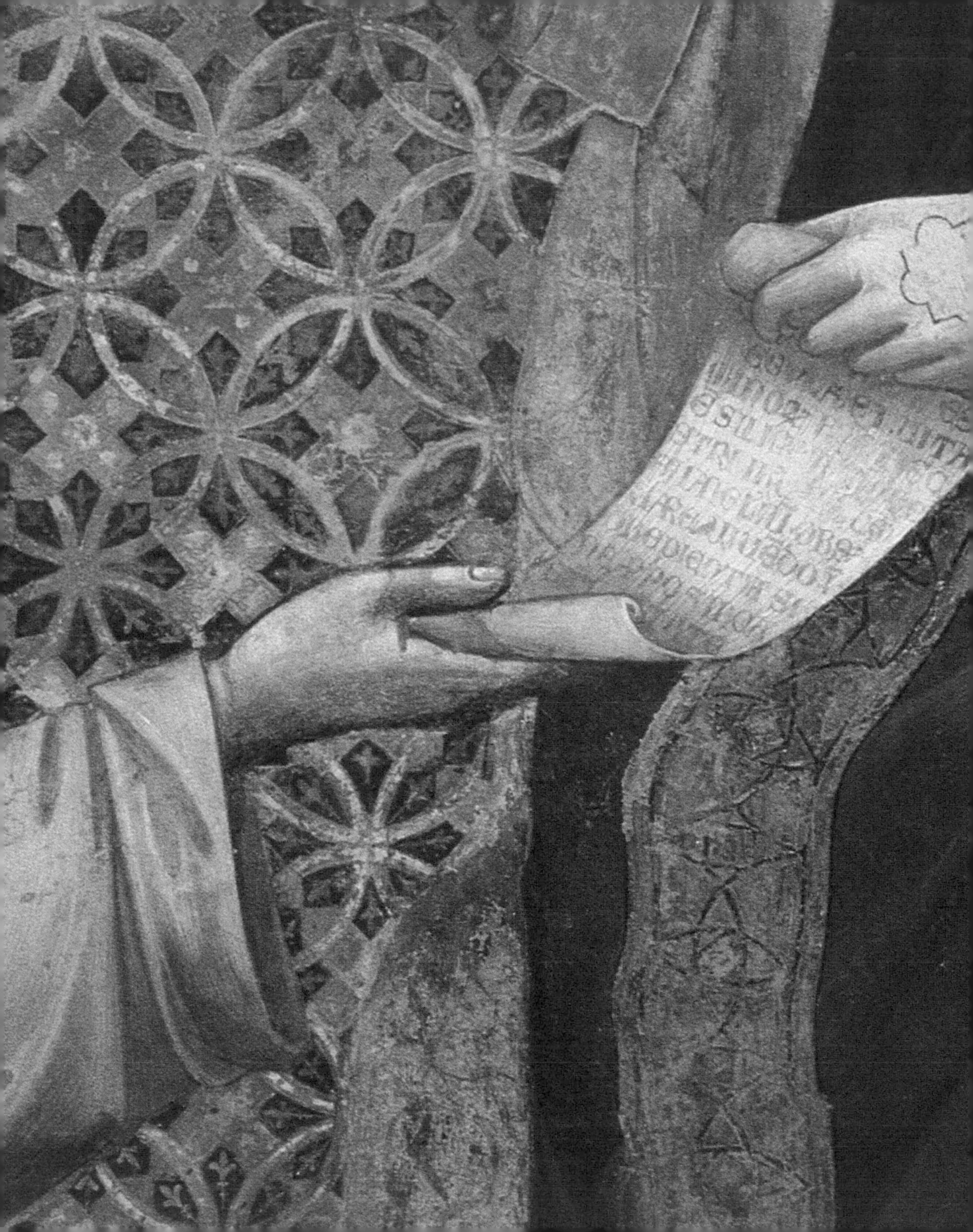

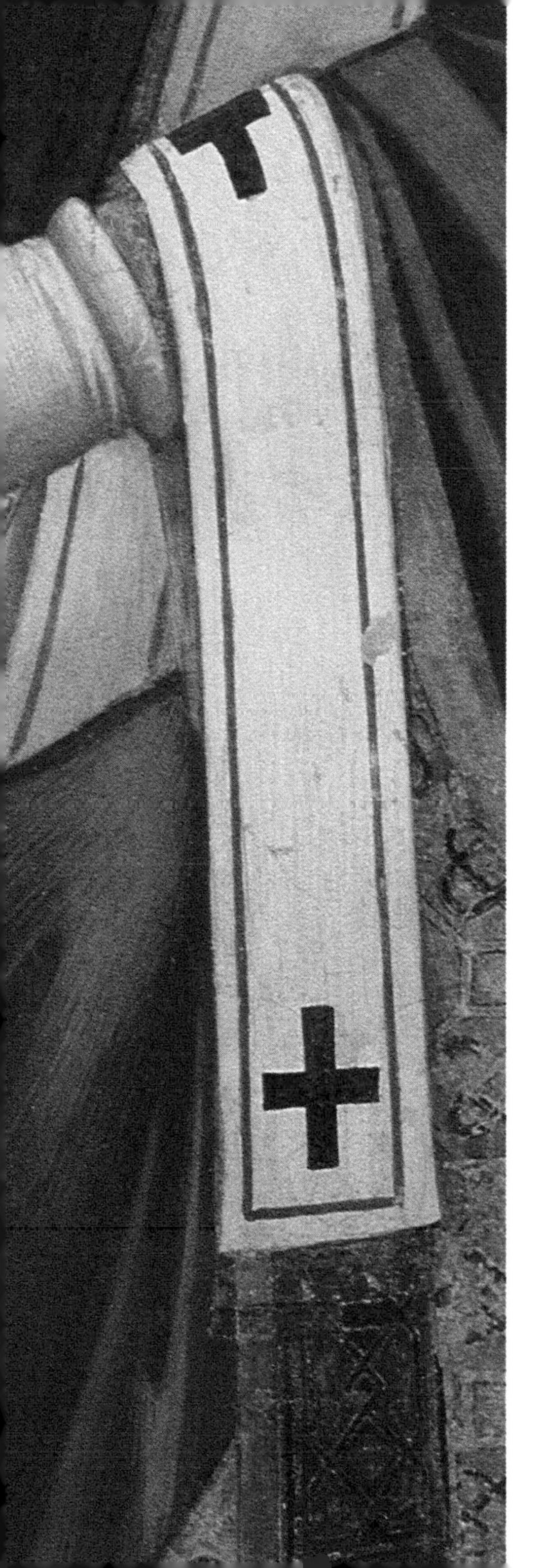

A Holy Contract

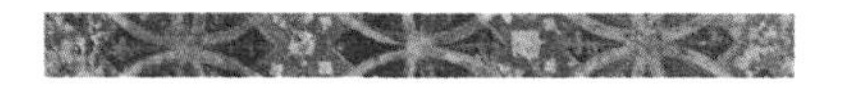

At times the saint would repeat: "In as far as the brothers depart from poverty, in so much will the world depart from them, and they will seek," he said, "and not find. But if they embrace my Lady Poverty, the world will provide for them, because they have been given to the world unto its salvation." And again: "There is a contract between the world and the brothers: the brothers must give the world a good example, the world must provide for their needs. When they break faith and withdraw their good example, the world will withdraw its hand in a just censure."

(Thomas of Celano, *The Second Life of St Francis,* Ch. XL, No. 70)

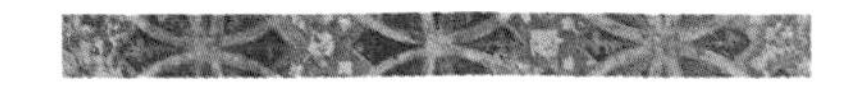

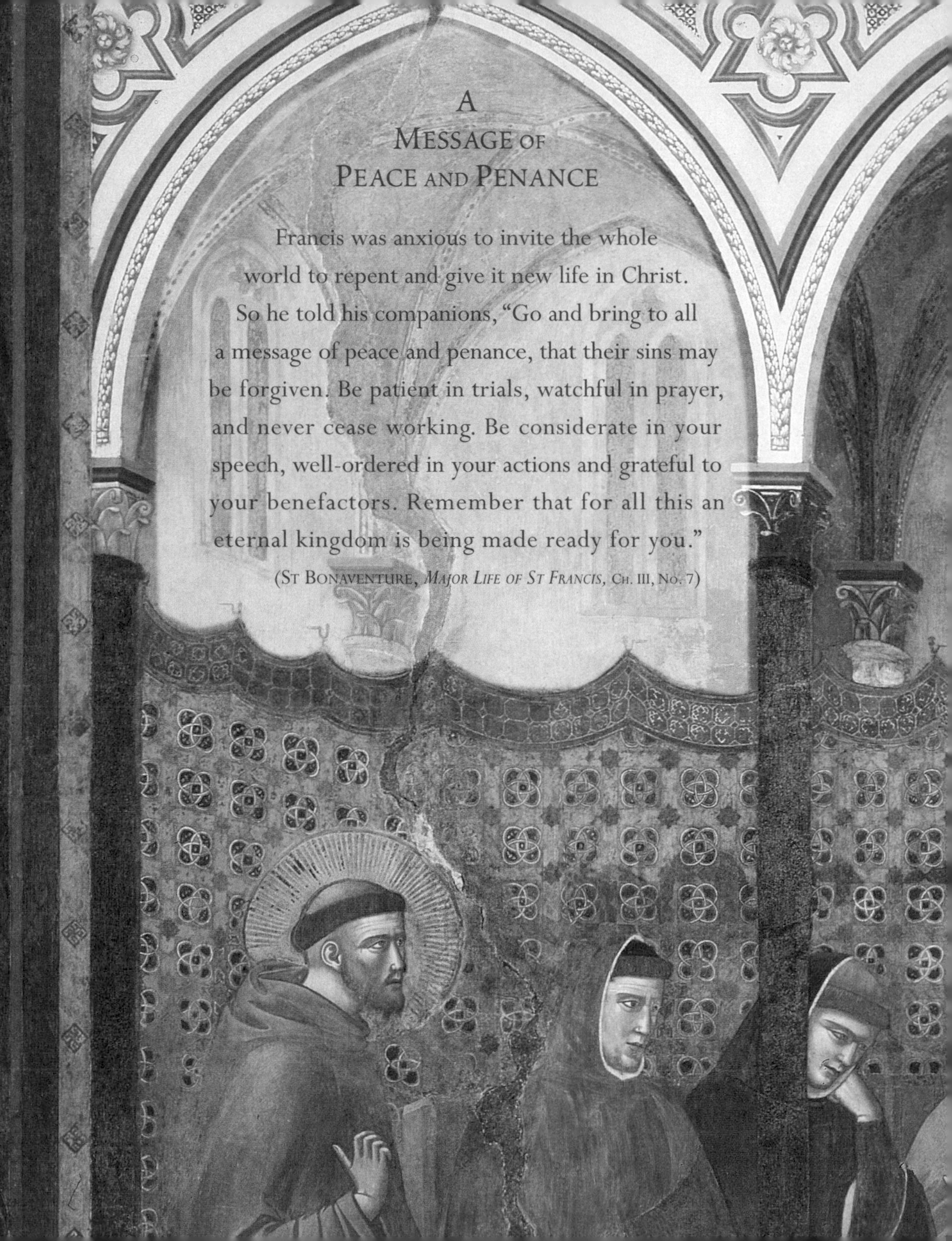

A Message of Peace and Penance

Francis was anxious to invite the whole world to repent and give it new life in Christ. So he told his companions, "Go and bring to all a message of peace and penance, that their sins may be forgiven. Be patient in trials, watchful in prayer, and never cease working. Be considerate in your speech, well-ordered in your actions and grateful to your benefactors. Remember that for all this an eternal kingdom is being made ready for you."

(St Bonaventure, *Major Life of St Francis*, Ch. III, No. 7)

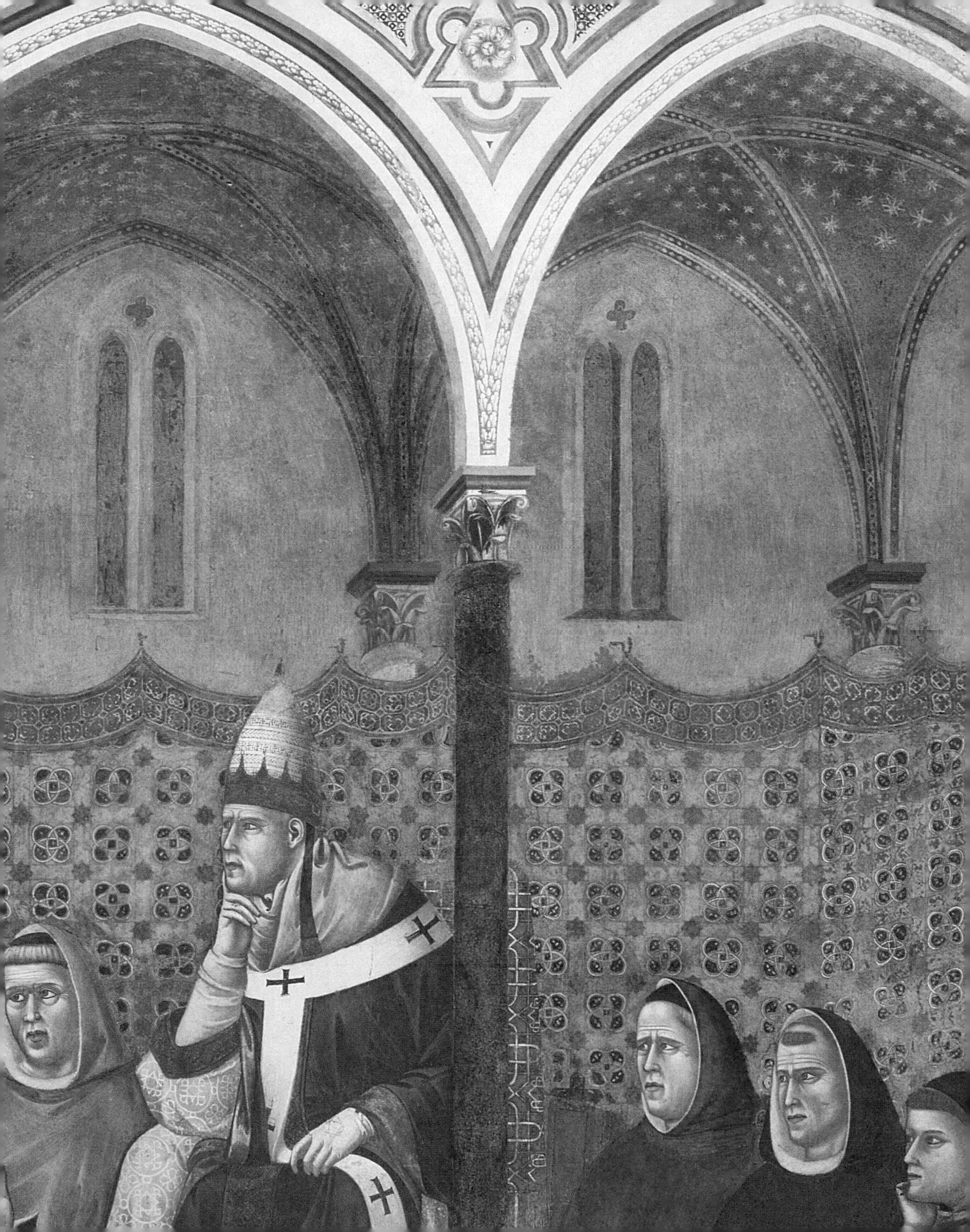

Patience

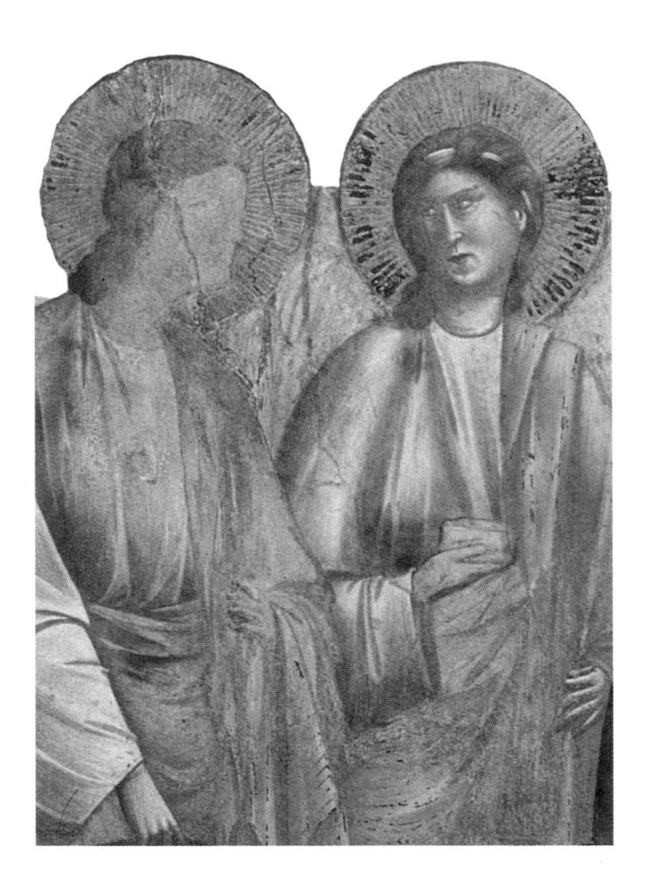

We can never tell how patient or humble a person is when everything is going well with him. But when those who should co-operate with him do the exact opposite, then we can tell. A man has as much patience and humility as he has then, and no more.

(*The Admonitions*, XIII)

True Love

Blessed that friar who loves his brother as much when he is sick and can be of no use to him as when he is well and can be of use to him. Blessed that friar who loves and respects his brother as much when he is absent as when he is present and who would not say anything behind his back that he could not say charitably to his face.

(*The Admonitions*, XXV)

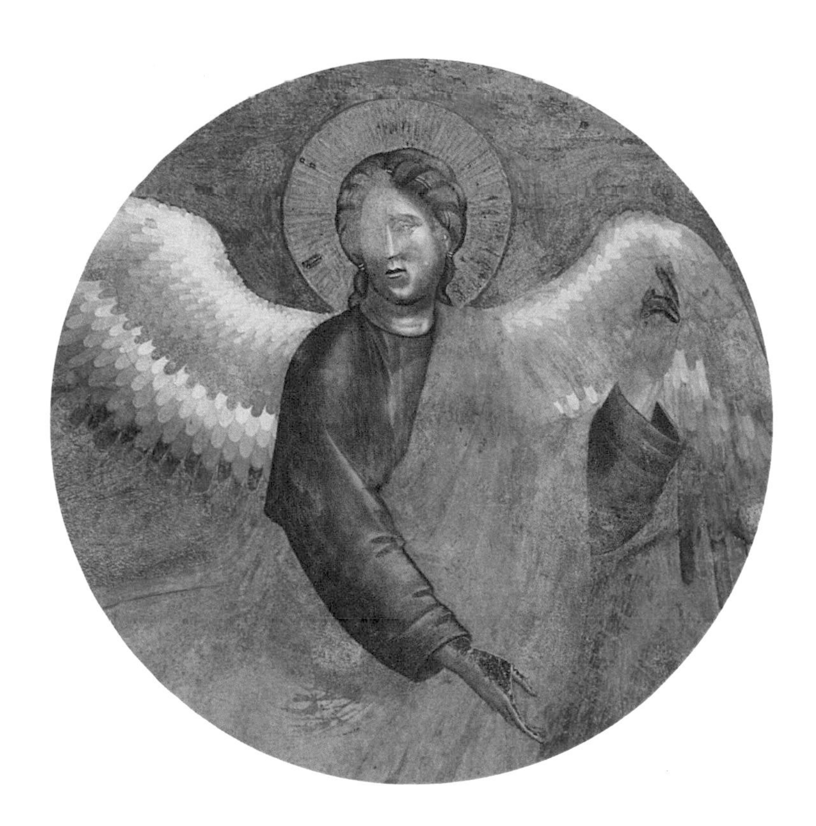

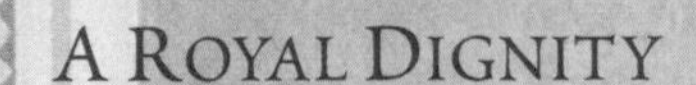

A Royal Dignity

The Lord is well pleased with poverty, and above all with that poverty that is voluntary. For I have a royal dignity and a special nobility, namely, to follow the Lord who, *being rich, became poor for us*. I get more delight from a poor table that is furnished with small alms than from great tables on which dainty foods are placed almost without number.

(Thomas of Celano, *The Second Life of St Francis,* Ch. XLIII, No. 73)

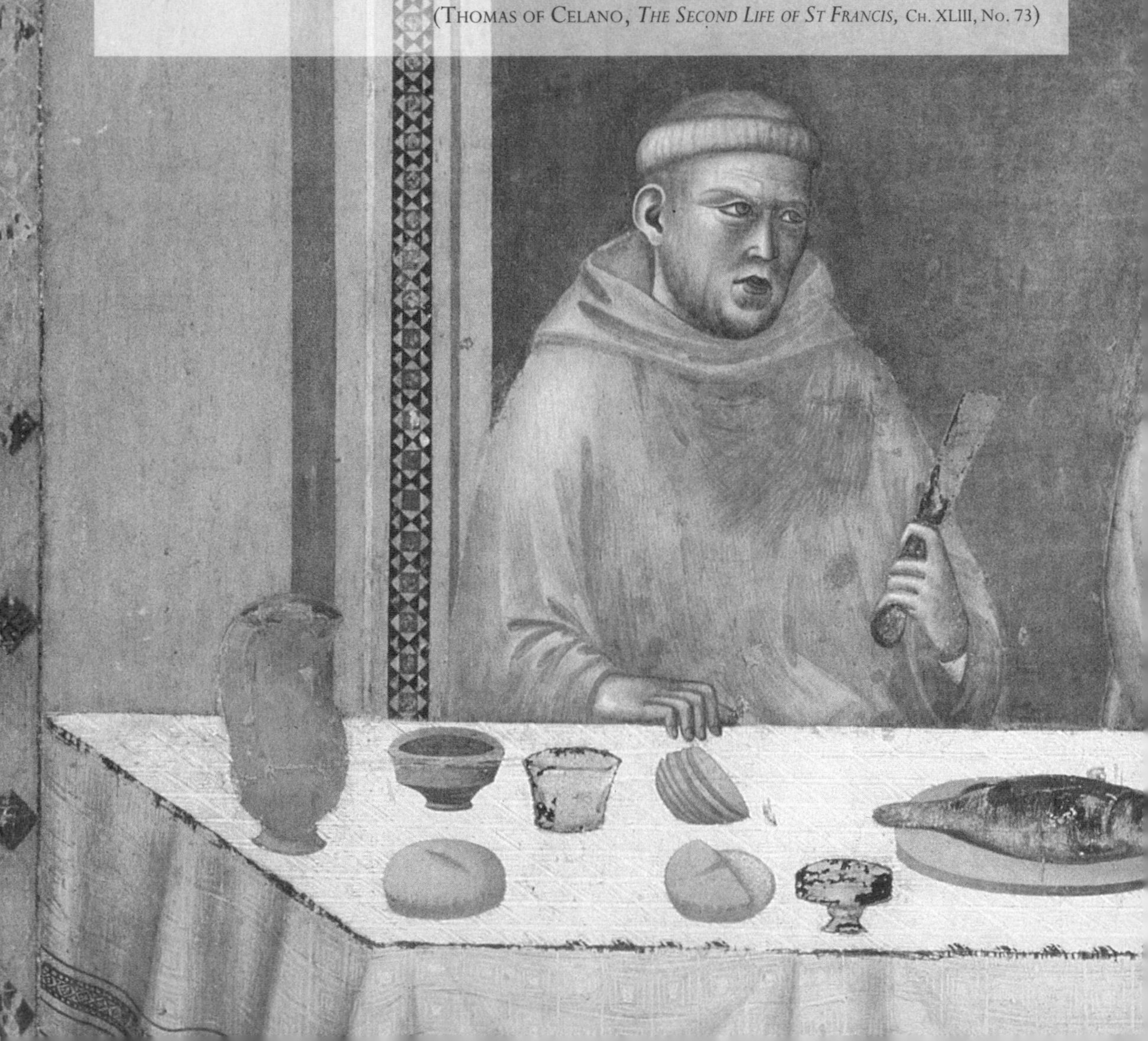

On the Perfect Way of Obedience

The most holy Father used to say to his friars, "Dearest brothers, carry out an order at once, and don't wait for it to be repeated. Don't plead or object that anything in a command is impossible, for if I were to order you to do something beyond your strength, holy obedience would not fail to support you."

(*Mirror of Perfection*, 47)

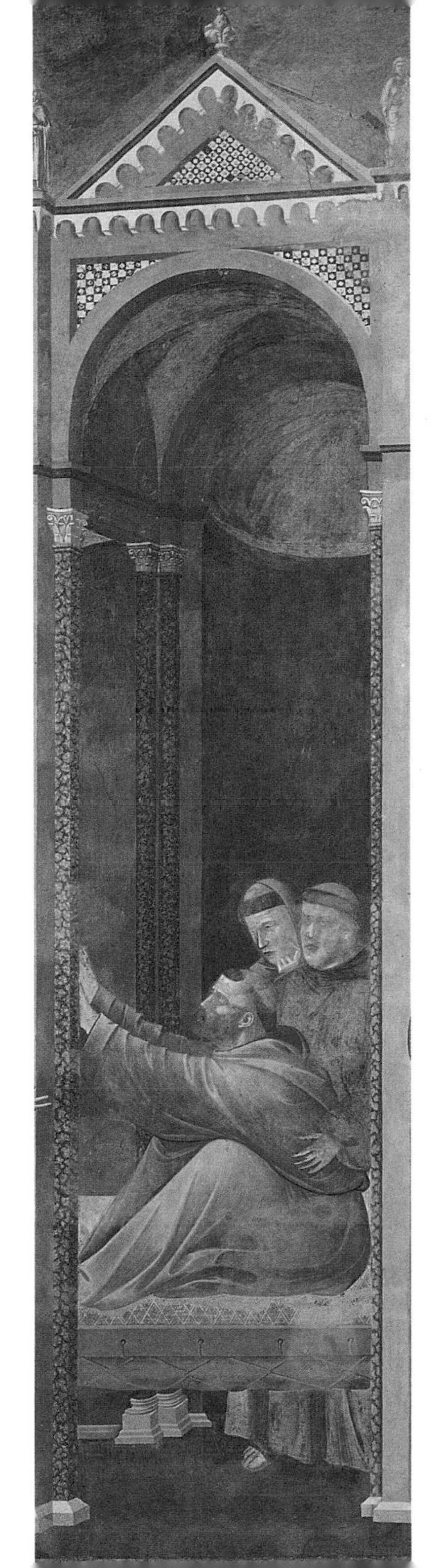

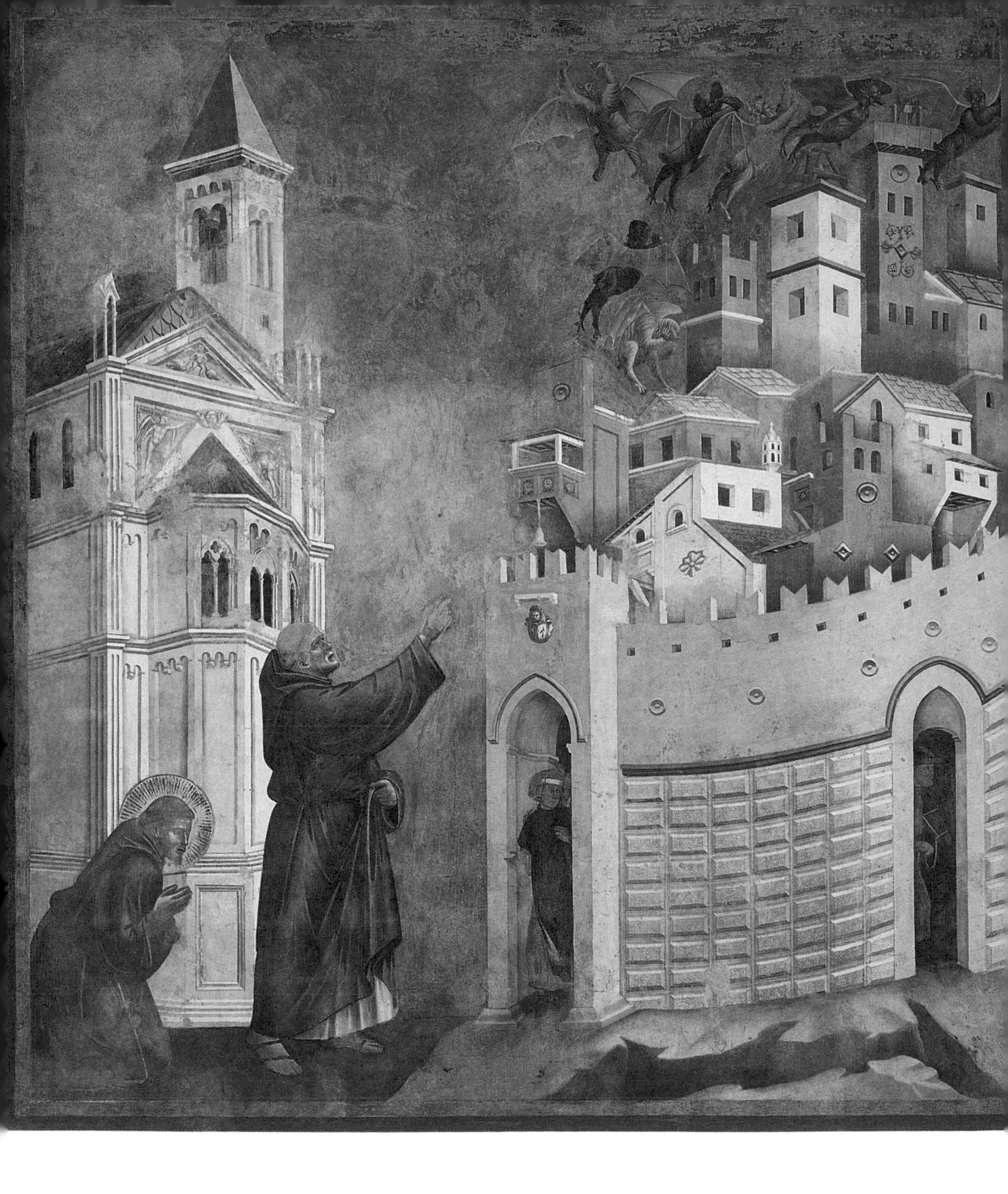

The Expulsion of the Devils from Arezzo

On (one) occasion St Francis arrived at Arezzo when the whole town was being torn with faction fights and threatened with destruction. There he was given hospitality in a village near the town and he could see the devils rejoicing over it and urging the people on to mutual slaughter. He was anxious to put the malicious powers of evil to flight and so he sent brother Silvester, who was a man of dove-like simplicity, telling him to approach the town like a herald. "Go up to the town gate," he said, "and in the name of almighty God command the devils in virtue of obedience to go away immediately." Silvester was a genuinely obedient man and did what he was told. There and then the town was restored to peace and the townspeople set about reforming the laws governing their mutual rights peacefully. Once the malignant and presumptuous influence of the demons which encompassed the town like a besieging army had been counteracted, it needed only the wisdom of a beggar, that is, Francis' humility, to restore peace and save the day. By the heroic practice of humble obedience Francis had gained complete authority over the rebellious spirits, so that he could crush their frantic efforts and put an end to the violence they attempted.

(St Bonaventure, *Major Life of St Francis*, Ch. VI, No. 9)

A True and Humble Faith

Nothing, then, must keep us back, nothing separate us from him, nothing come between us and him. At all times and seasons, in every country and place, every day and all day, we must have a true and humble faith, and keep him in our hearts where we must love, honour, adore, serve, praise and bless, glorify and acclaim, magnify and thank, the most high supreme and eternal God, Three and One, Father, Son and Holy Spirit, Creator of all and Saviour of those who believe in him, who hope in him, and who love him; without beginning and without end, he is unchangeable, invisible, indescribable and ineffable, incomprehensible, unfathomable, blessed and worthy of all praise.

(*Rule of 1221*, Ch. XXIII)

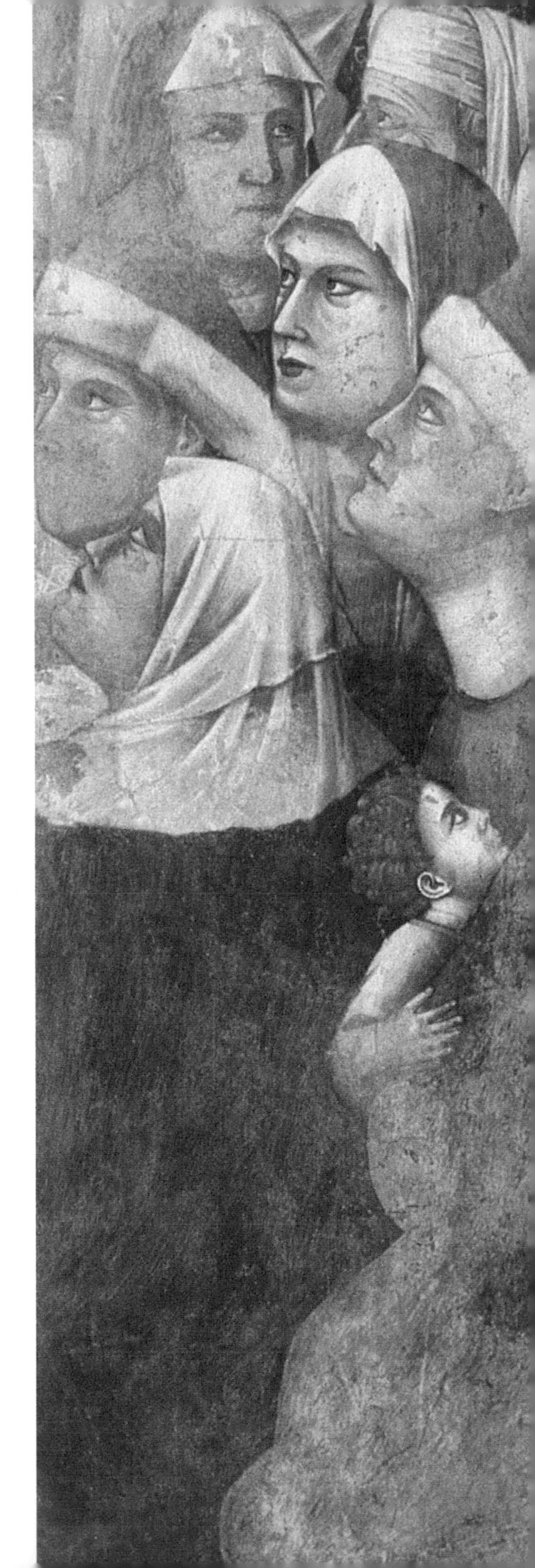

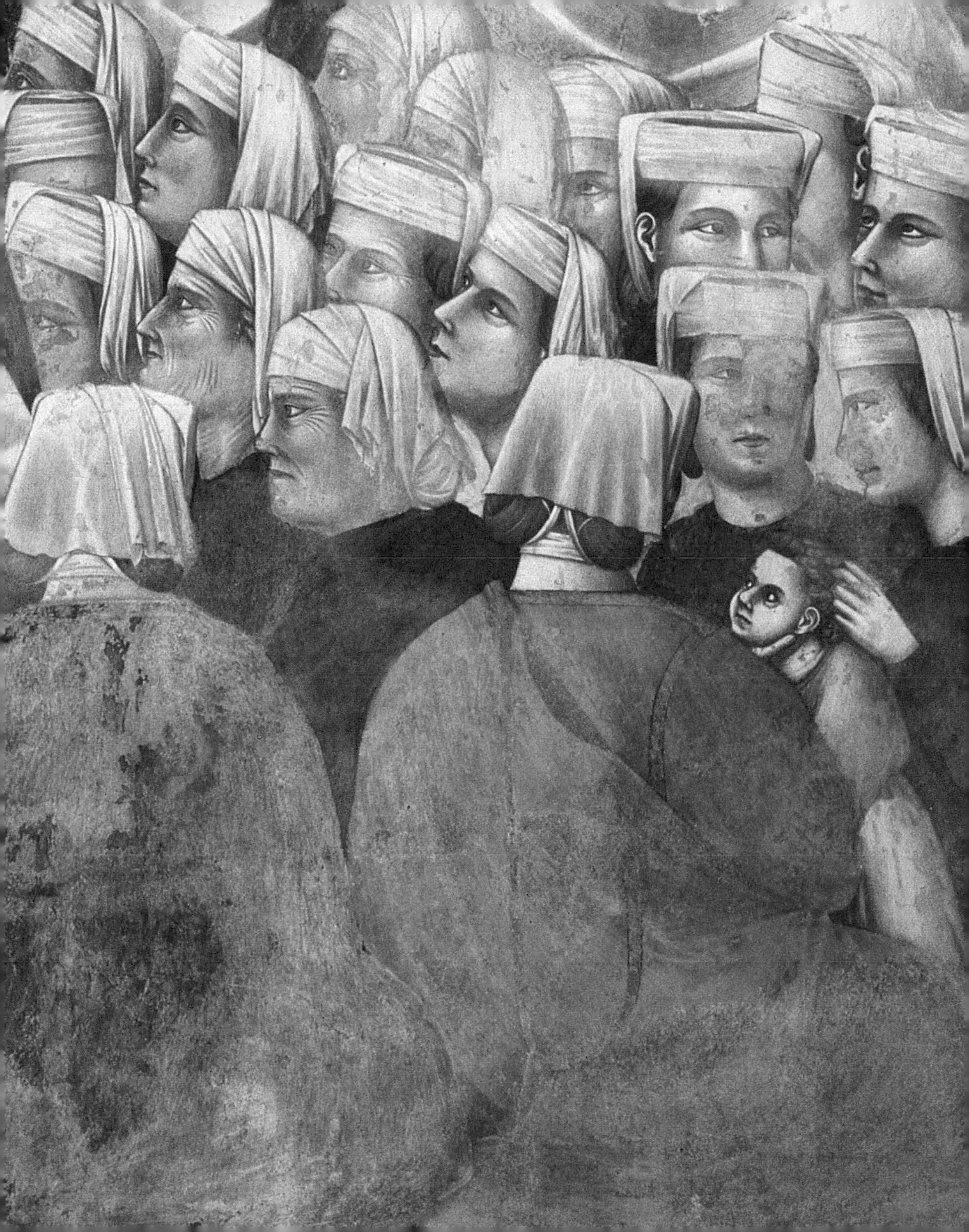

The Canticle of Brother Sun

Most high, all-powerful, all good, Lord!
All praise is yours, all glory, all honour
And all blessing.
To you, alone, Most High, do they belong.
Nor mortal lips are worthy
To pronounce your name.
All praise be yours, my Lord, through all that you have made,
And first my lord Brother Sun,
Who brings the day; and the light you give to us through him.
How beautiful is he, how radiant in all his splendour!
Of you, Most High, he bears the likeness.
All praise be yours, my Lord, through Sister Moon and Stars,
In the heavens you have made them, bright
And precious and fair.
All praise be yours, my Lord, through Brothers Wind and Air,
And fair and stormy, all the weather's moods,
By which you cherish all that you have made.
All praise be yours, my Lord, through Sister Water,
So useful, lowly, precious and pure.
All praise be yours, my Lord, through Brother Fire,
Through whom you brighten up the night.
How beautiful is he, how gay! Full of power and strength.
All praise be yours, my Lord, through Sister Earth, our mother,
Who feeds us in her sovereignty and produces
Various fruits with coloured flowers and herbs.

All praise be yours, my Lord, through those who grant pardon
For love of you; through those who endure
Sickness and trial.
Happy those who endure in peace,
By you, Most High, they will be crowned.
All praise be yours, my Lord, through Sister Death,
From whose embrace no mortal can escape.
Woe to those who die in mortal sin!
Happy those She finds doing your will!
The second death can do no harm to them.
Praise and bless my Lord, and give him thanks,
And serve him with great humility.

(Writings of St Francis)

Anxieties and Worries

By the anxieties and worries of this life, the devil tries to dull our hearts and make a dwelling for himself there. And so we must all keep close watch over ourselves or we will be lost and turn our minds and hearts from God, because we think there is something worth having or doing, or that we will gain some advantage.

(*Rule of 1221*, Ch. XXII)

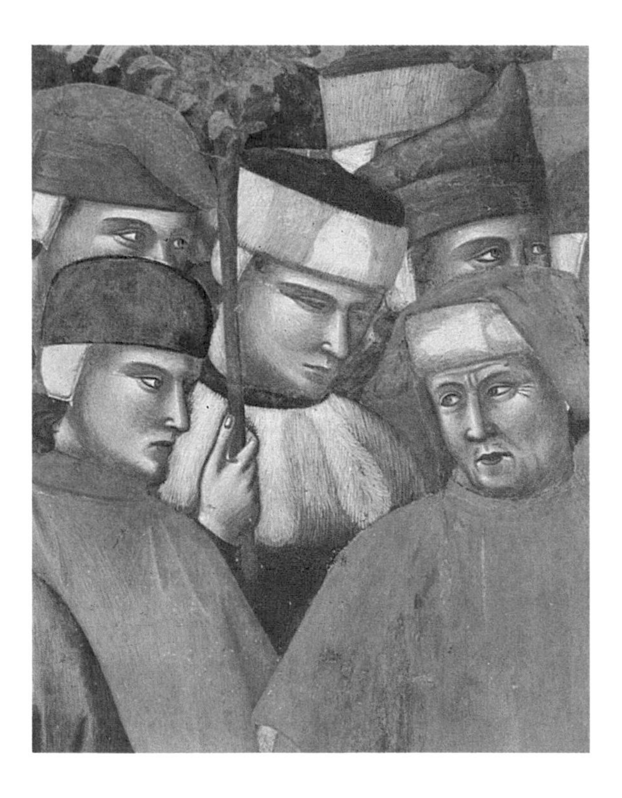

PRIVATE PRAYER

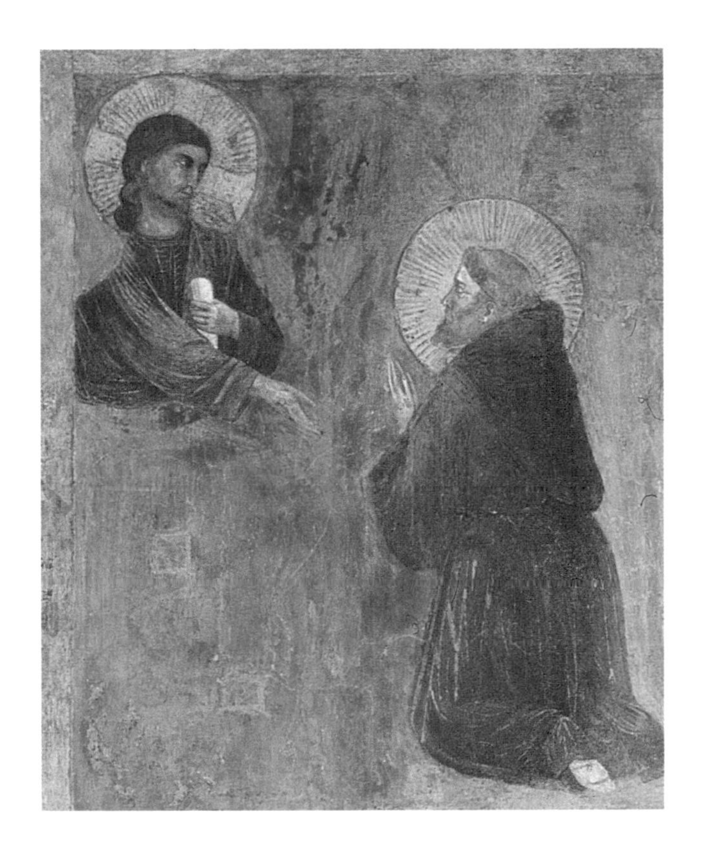

The brothers and sisters must guard with jealous watchfulness the times of private prayer. They must remember that corporate worship is not a substitute for the quiet communion of the individual soul with God.

(*The Principles*, SSF)

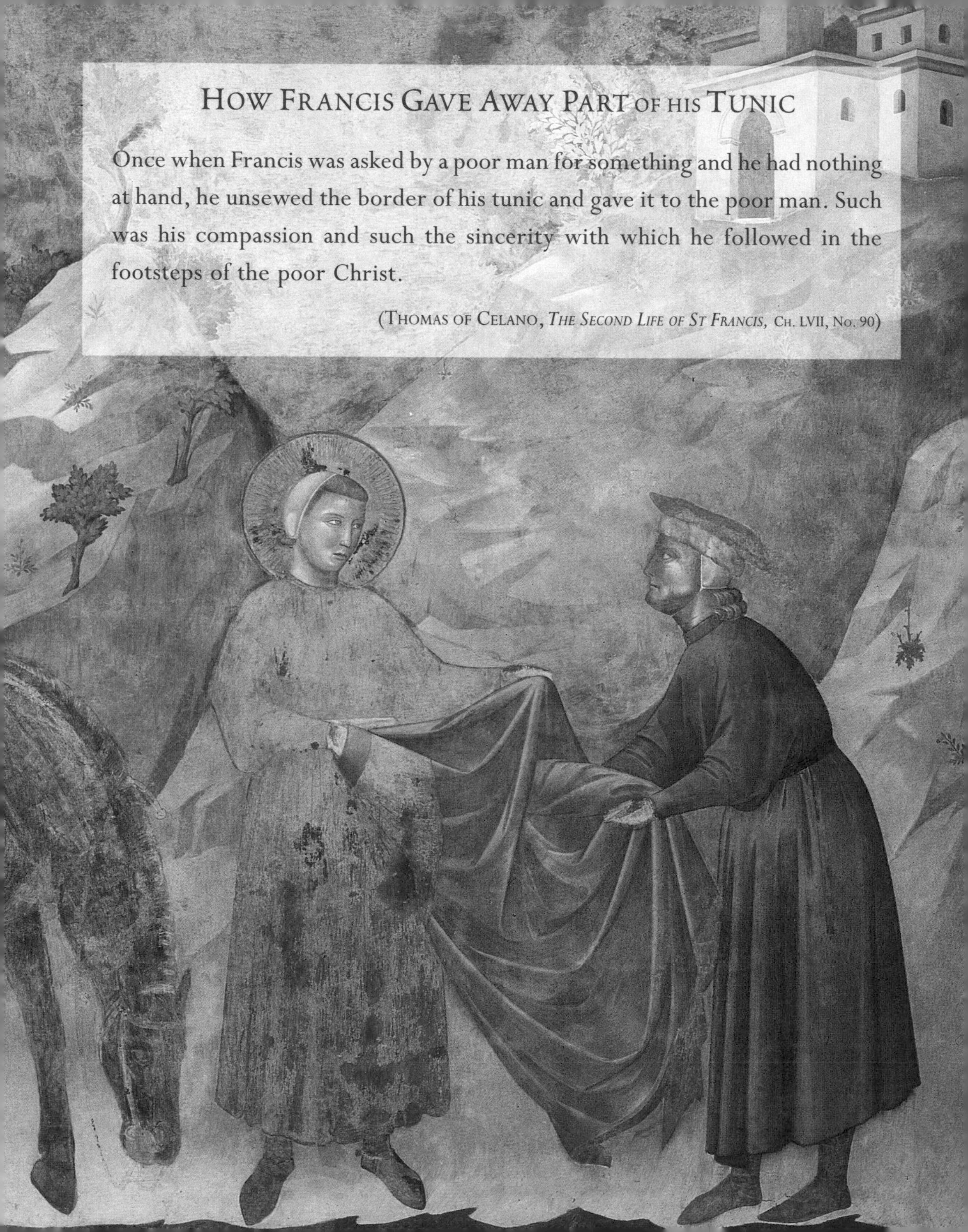

How Francis Gave Away Part of his Tunic

Once when Francis was asked by a poor man for something and he had nothing at hand, he unsewed the border of his tunic and gave it to the poor man. Such was his compassion and such the sincerity with which he followed in the footsteps of the poor Christ.

(Thomas of Celano, *The Second Life of St Francis,* Ch. LVII, No. 90)

JUDGING OTHERS

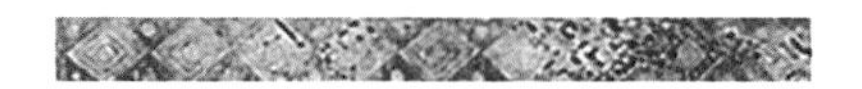

I warn all the friars and exhort them not to condemn or look down on people whom they see wearing soft or gaudy clothes and enjoying luxuries in food or drink; each one should rather condemn and despise himself.

(*RULE OF 1223*, CH. II)

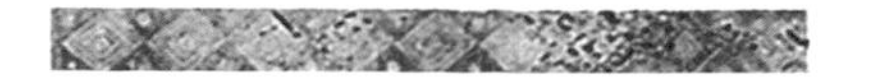

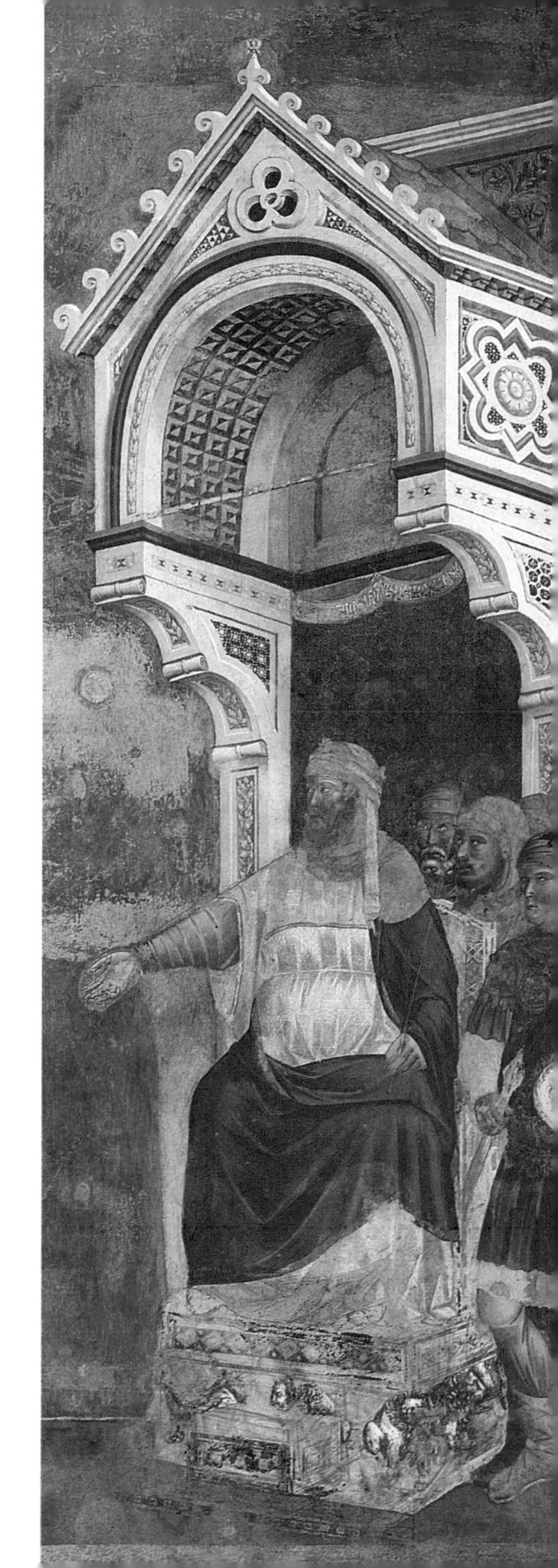

Francis Preaches to the Birds

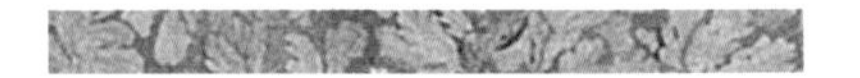

One time when Francis was walking with another friar in the Venetian marshes, they came upon a huge flock of birds, singing among the reeds. When he saw them, the saint said to his companion, "Our sisters the birds are praising their Creator. We will go in among them and sing God's praise, chanting the divine office." They went in among the birds which remained where they were, so that the friars could not hear themselves saying the office, they were making so much noise. Eventually the saint turned to them and said, "My sisters, stop singing until we have given God the praise to which he has a right." The birds were silent immediately and remained that way until Francis gave them permission to sing again, after they had taken plenty of time to say the office and had finished their praises. Then the birds began again, as usual.

(St Bonaventure, *Major Life of St Francis*, Ch. VIII, No. 9)

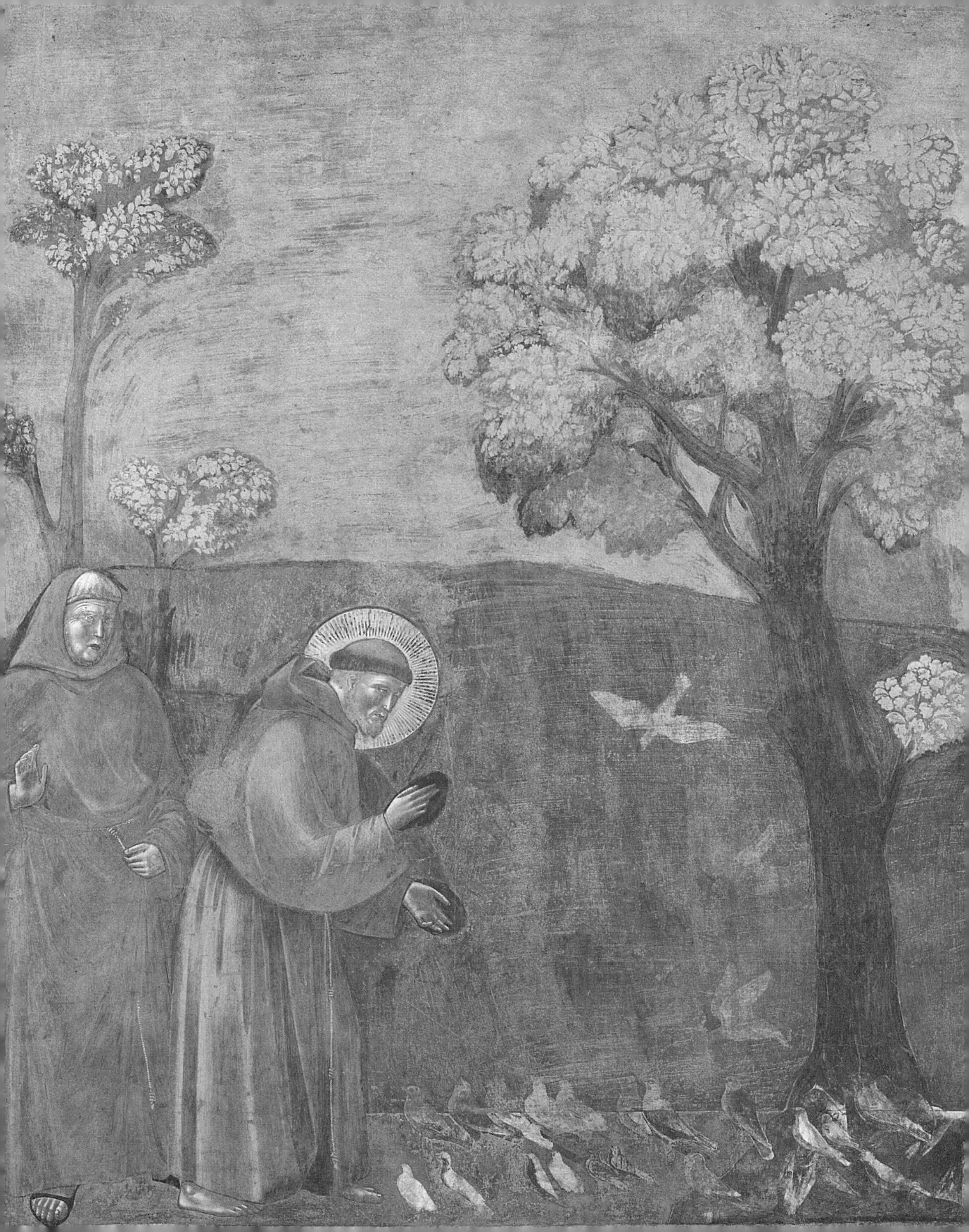

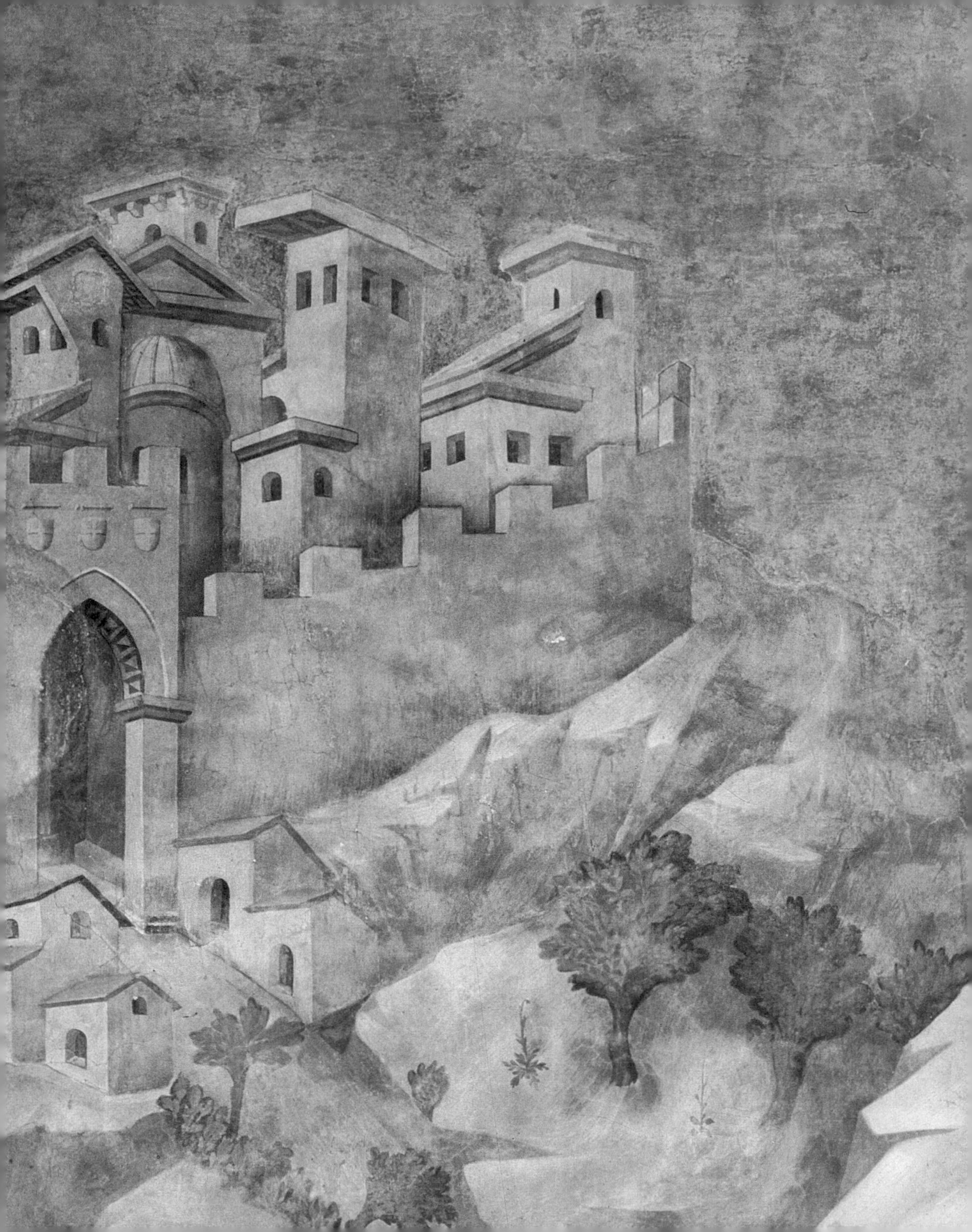

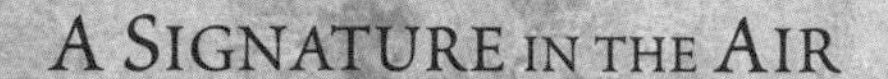

A Signature in the Air

Little lizards dart across the walls of Assisi, zigzagging quick patterns of their movements on tawny stone. Their green bodies against the pink and red made the whole wall interesting and alive.

Francis saw himself in these little creatures that shoot back and forth, in and out of the tiny crevices. They loved the geography of their little world and they went about the business of their lives unselfconsciously, totally preoccupied with the humble stone.

It was their movement that fascinated him. Their motion was a pattern scribbled in the air which disappeared as soon as it was made. There was no permanence in these tiny signatures, no monument to themselves left behind. That is what he wanted to be: a tiny signature in the air that thrilled someone who saw it, but was as anonymous as a lizard's zigzagged darting on a pink Assisi wall. His movement would be his poem.

(Murray Bodo, *The Journey and the Dream*)

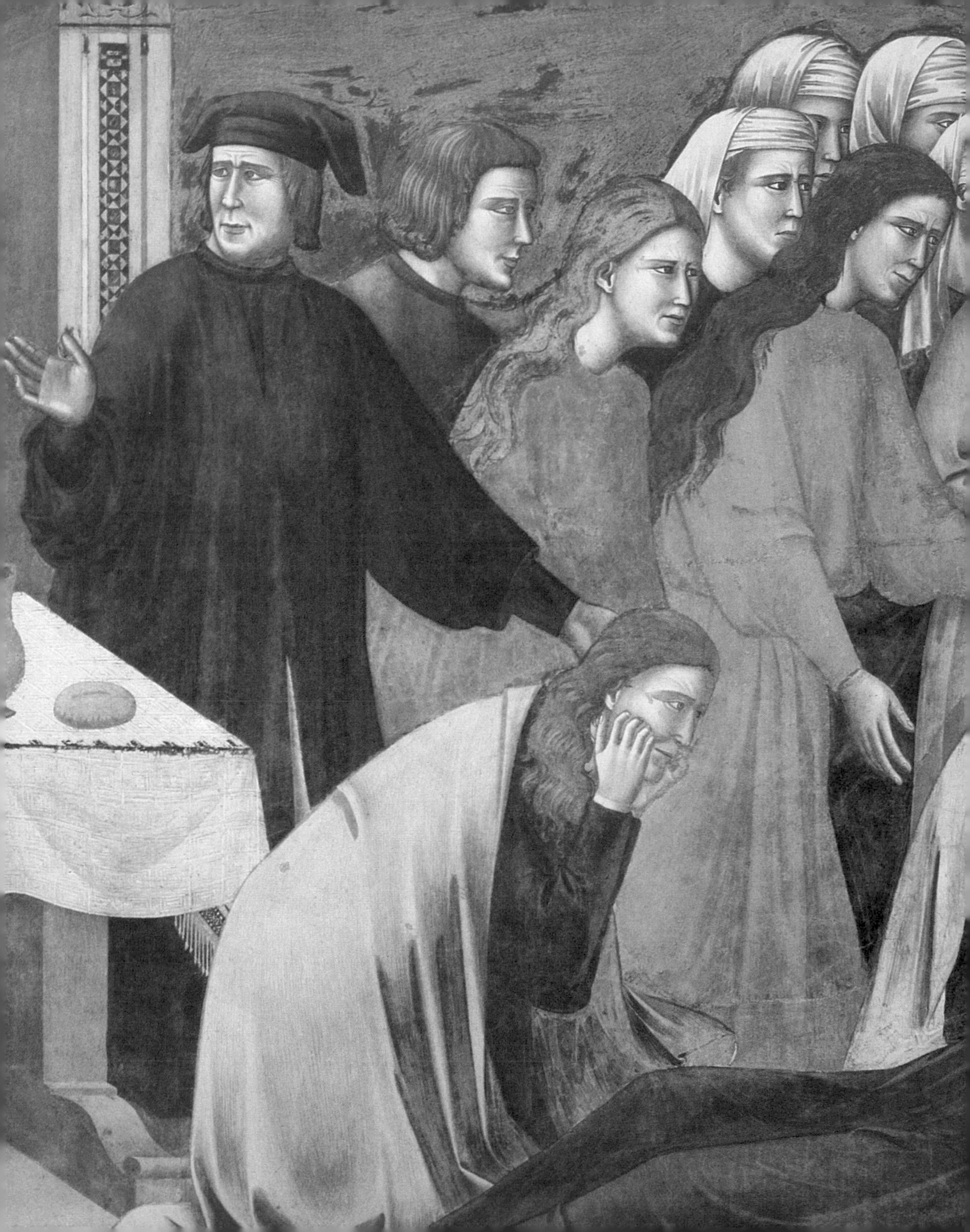

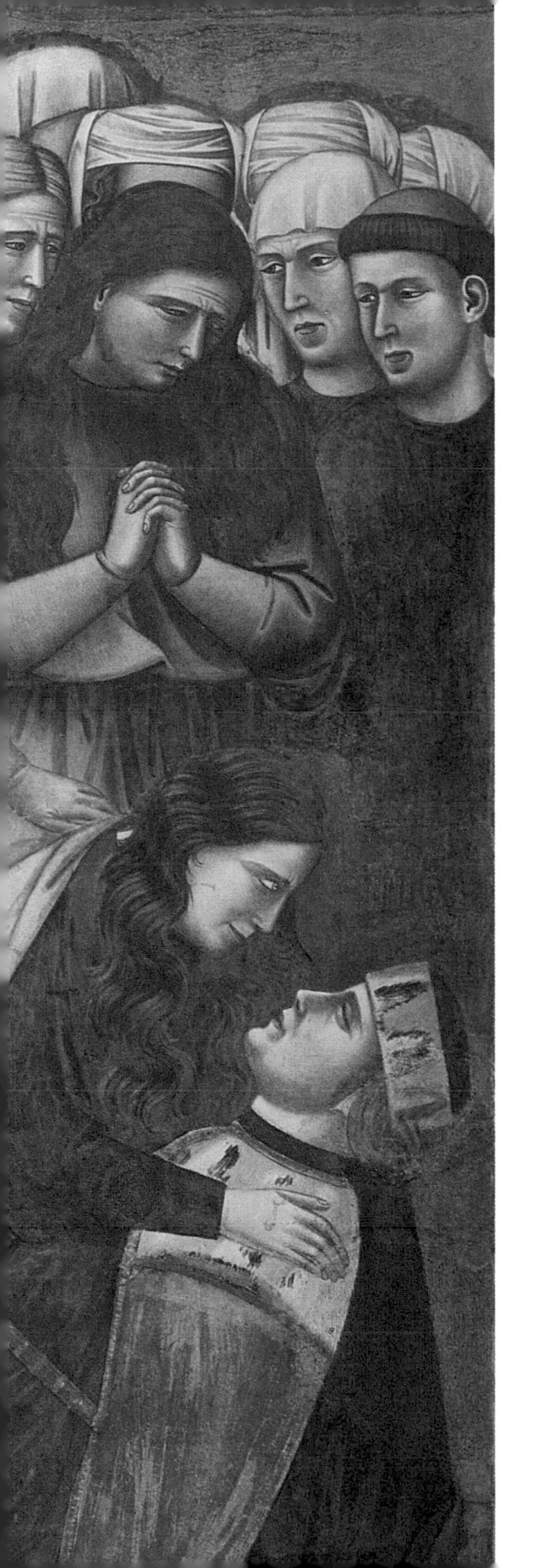

Our Haven and Our Hope

You are love,
　　You are wisdom.
　　You are humility,
　　You are endurance.
　　You are rest,
　　You are peace.
　　You are joy and gladness.
　　You are justice and moderation.
　　You are all our riches,
　　And you suffice for us.
You are beauty.
　　You are gentleness.
　　You are our protector,
　　You are our guardian and defender.
　　You are our courage.
　　You are our haven and our hope.
You are our faith,
　　Our great consolation.
　　You are our eternal life,
　　Great and wonderful Lord,
　　God almighty,
　　Merciful Saviour.

(*Praises of God*)

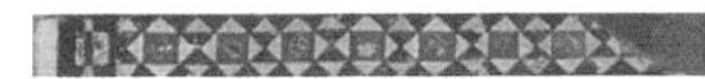

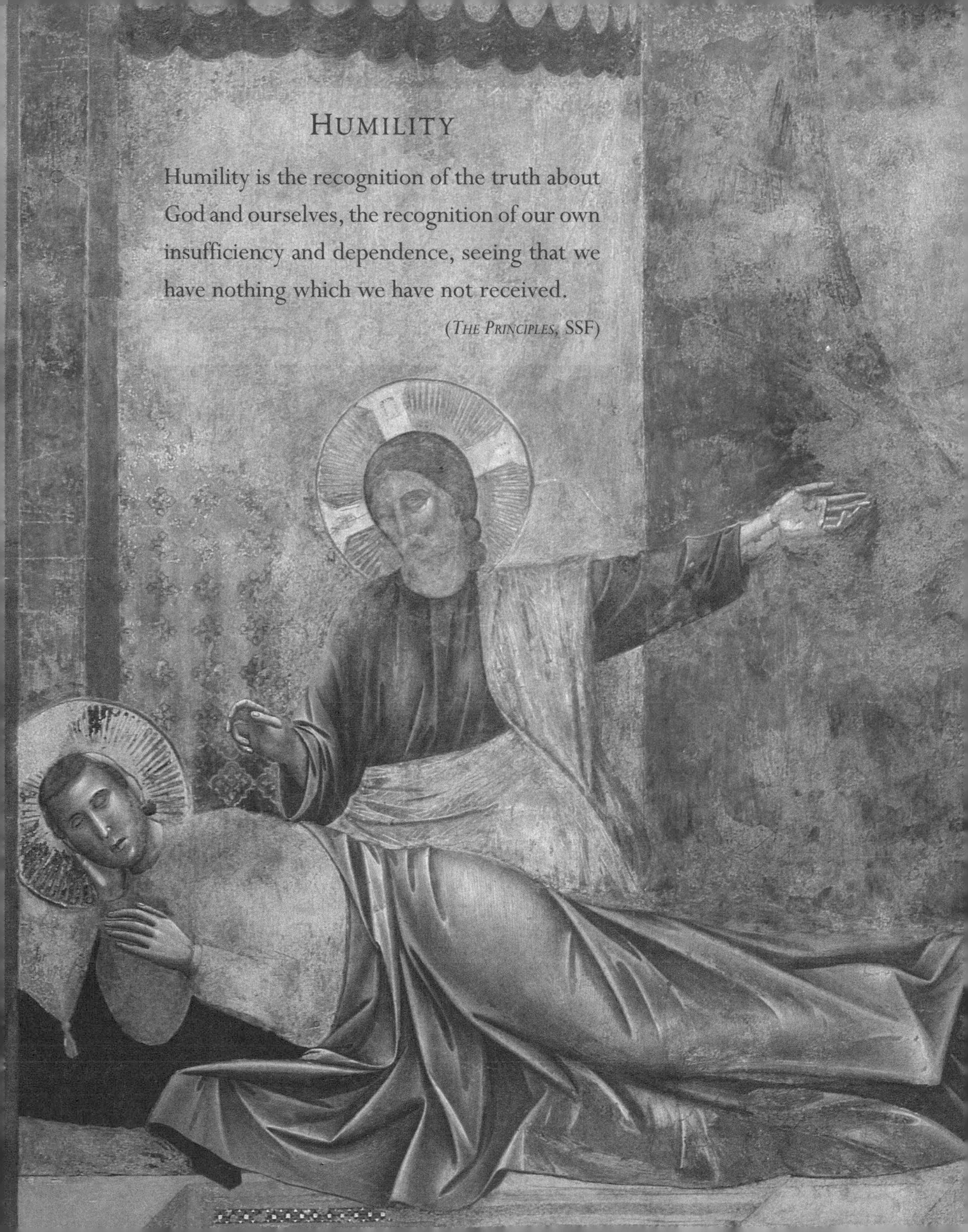

Humility

Humility is the recognition of the truth about God and ourselves, the recognition of our own insufficiency and dependence, seeing that we have nothing which we have not received.

(*The Principles,* SSF)

Travelling Pilgrims

The friars should be delighted to follow the lowliness and poverty of our Lord Jesus Christ, remembering that of the whole world we must own nothing*; but having food and sufficient clothing, with these let us be content*, as St Paul says. They should be glad to live among social outcasts, among the poor and helpless, the sick and the lepers, and those who beg by the wayside. If they are in want, they should not be ashamed to beg alms.

(*Rule of 1221*, Ch. IX)

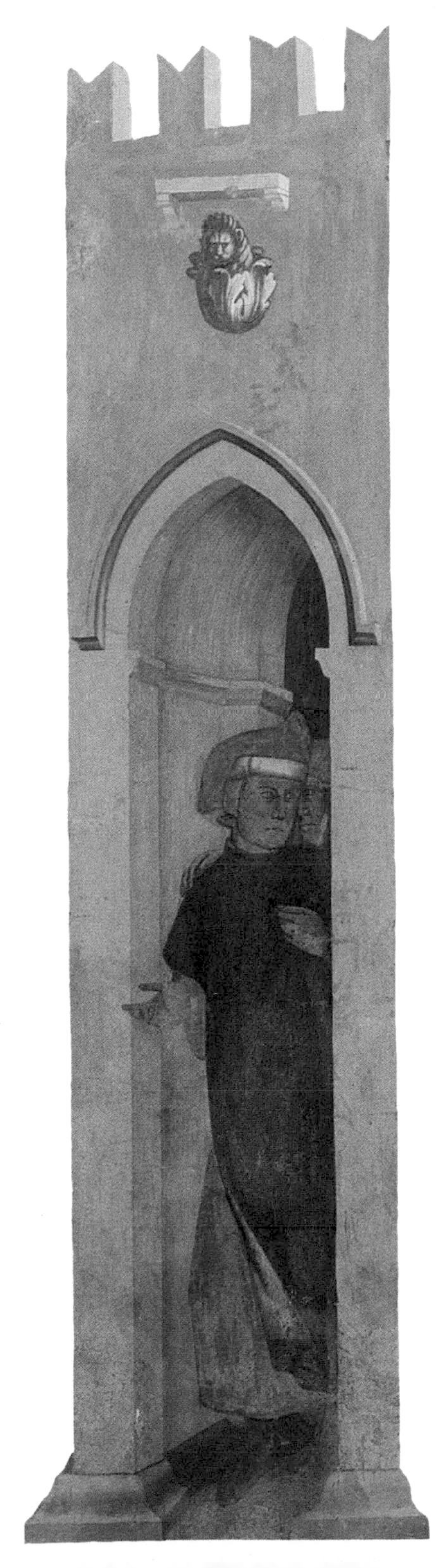

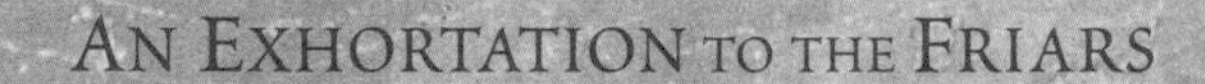

An Exhortation to the Friars

In that love which is God, I entreat all my friars, ministers and subjects, to put away every attachment, all care and solicitude, and serve, love, honour, and adore our Lord and God with a pure heart and mind; this is what he seeks above all else. We should make a dwelling-place within ourselves where he can stay, he who is God almighty, Father, Son and Holy Spirit.

(*Rule of 1221*, Ch. XXII)

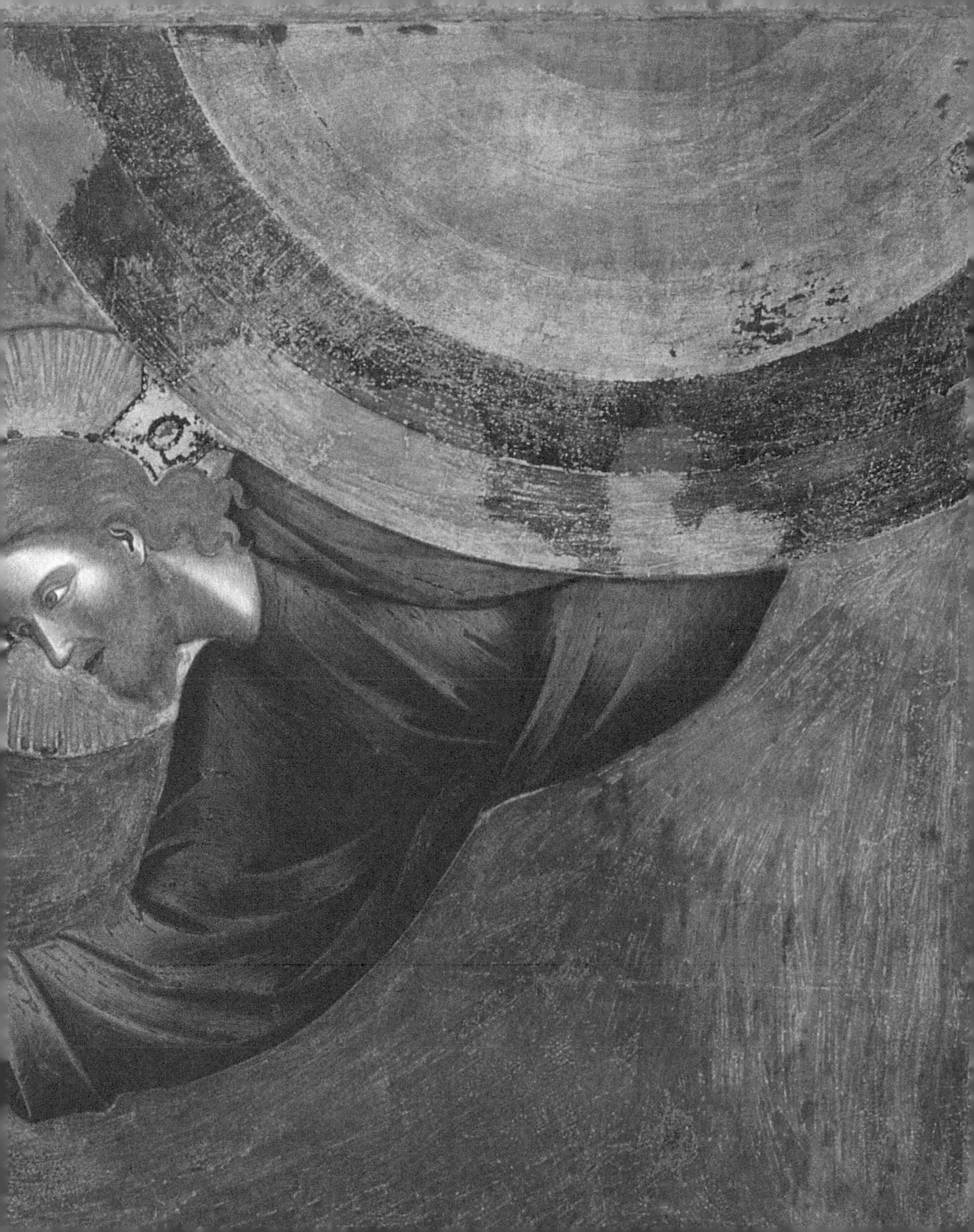

True Correction

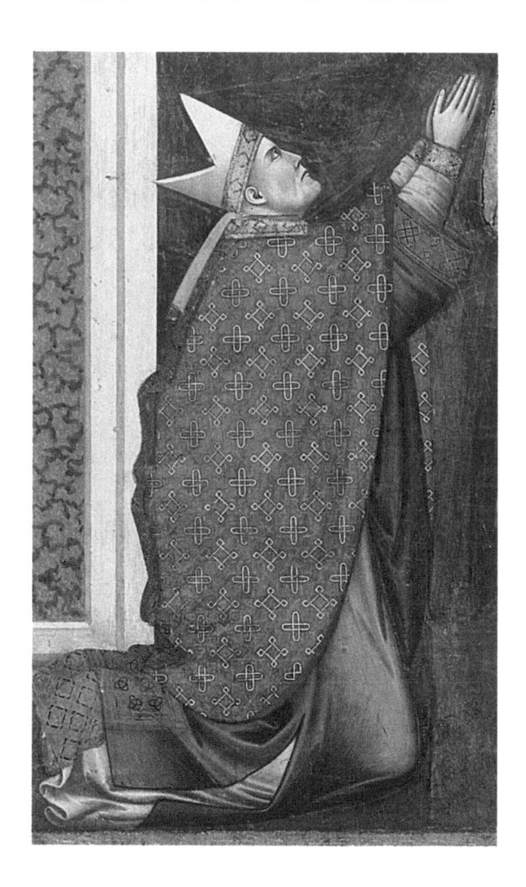

Blessed that religious who takes blame, accusation, or punishment from another as patiently as if it were coming from himself. Blessed the religious who obeys quietly when he is corrected, confesses his fault humbly and makes atonement cheerfully. Blessed the religious who is in no hurry to make excuses, but accepts the embarrassment and blame for some fault he did not commit.

(*The Admonitions*, XXIII)

Charity

Our Lord says in the Gospel, *Love your enemies*. A man really loves his enemy when he is not offended by the injury done to himself, but for love of God feels burning sorrow for the sin his enemy has brought on his own soul, and proves his love in a practical way.

(*The Admonitions*, IX)

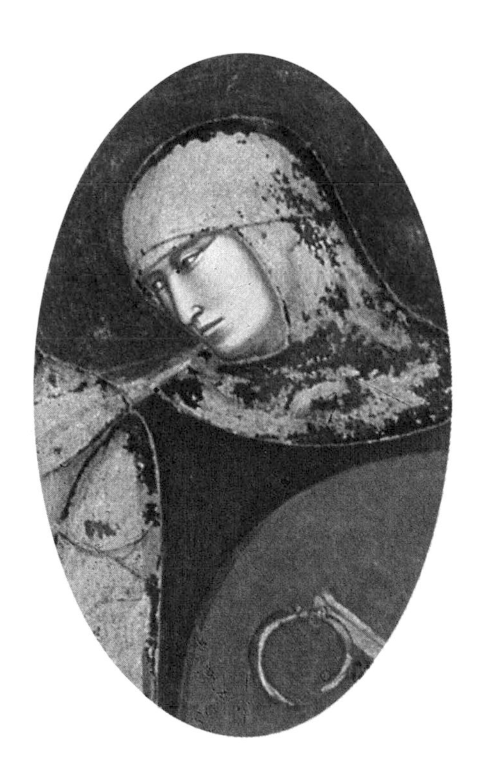

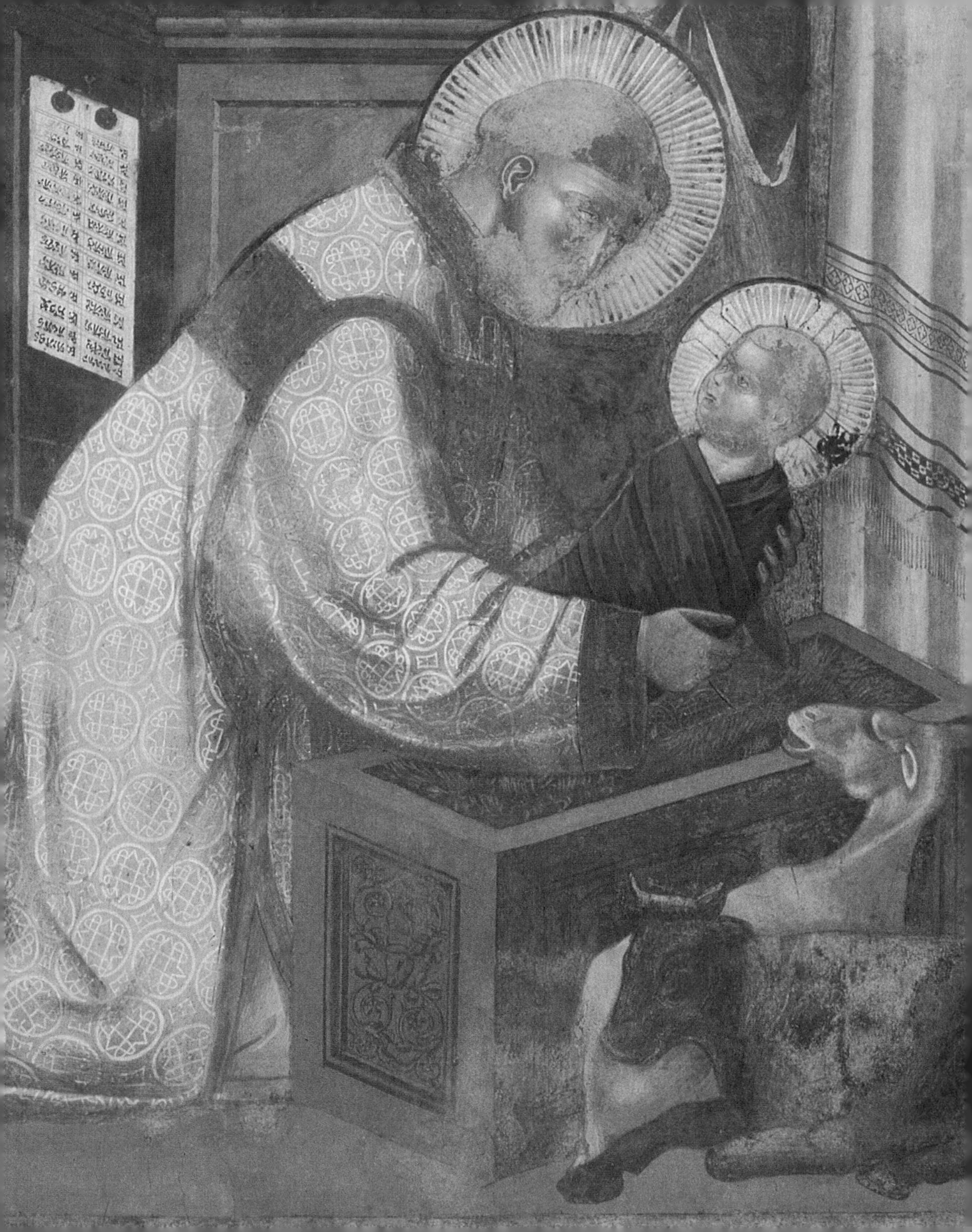

The First Crib at Greccio

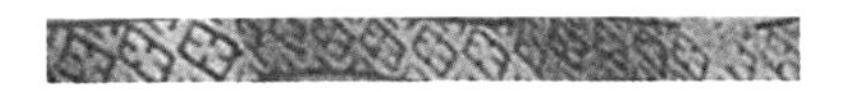

"I wish to do something that will recall to memory the little Child who was born in Bethlehem and set before our bodily eyes in some way the inconveniences of his infant needs, how he lay in a manger, how, with an ox and an ass standing by, he lay upon the hay where he had been placed." When the good and faithful man heard these things, he ran with haste and prepared in that place all the things the saint had told him.

But the day of joy drew near, the time of great rejoicing came. The brothers were called from their various places. Men and women of that neighbourhood prepared with glad hearts, according to their means, candles and torches to light up that night that has lighted up all the days and years with its gleaming star. At length the saint of God came, and finding all things prepared, *he saw it and was glad*. The manger was prepared, the hay had been brought, the ox and ass were led in. There simplicity was honoured, poverty was exalted, humility was commended, and Greccio was made, as it were, a new Bethlehem. The night was lighted up like the day, and it delighted men and beasts. The people came and were filled with new joy over the new mystery. The woods rang with the voices of the crowd and the rocks made answer to their jubilation. The brothers sang, paying their debt of praise to the Lord, and the whole night resounded with their rejoicing. The saint of God stood before the manger, uttering sighs, overcome with love, and filled with a wonderful happiness.

(Thomas of Celano, *The First Life of St Francis,* Ch. XXX, Nos. 84-85)

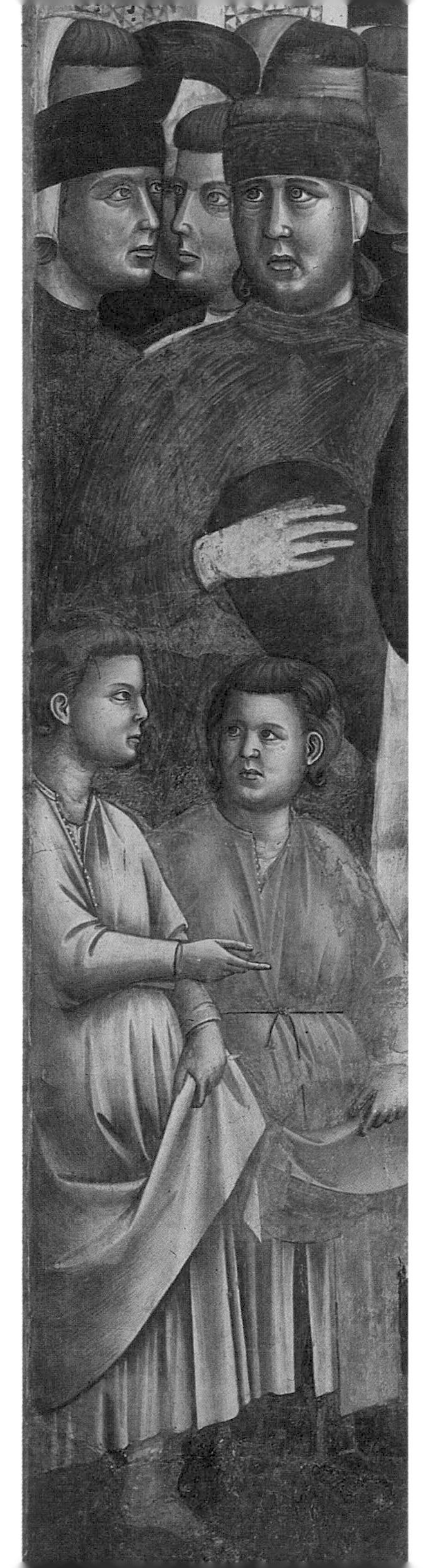

Brothers Sun and Fire

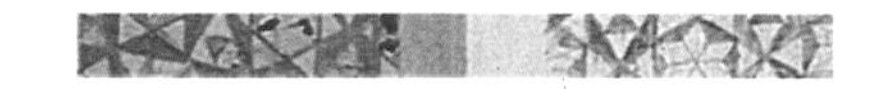

At dawn, when the sun rises, all men should praise God, who created him for our use, and through him gives light to our eyes by day. And at nightfall every man should praise God for Brother Fire, by whom he gives light to our eyes in the darkness. For we are all blind, and by these two brothers of ours God gives light to our eyes, so we should give special praise to our Creator for these and other creatures that serve us day by day.

(*Mirror of Perfection*, 119)

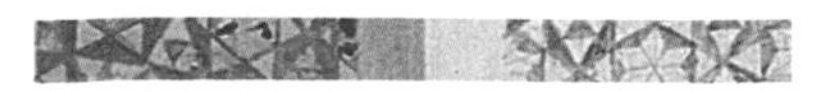

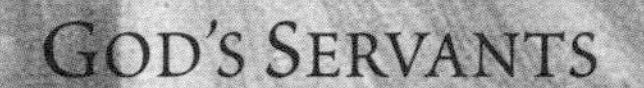

God's Servants

What are God's servants but his minstrels, who must inspire the hearts of men and stir them to spiritual joy.

(*Mirror of Perfection*, 100)

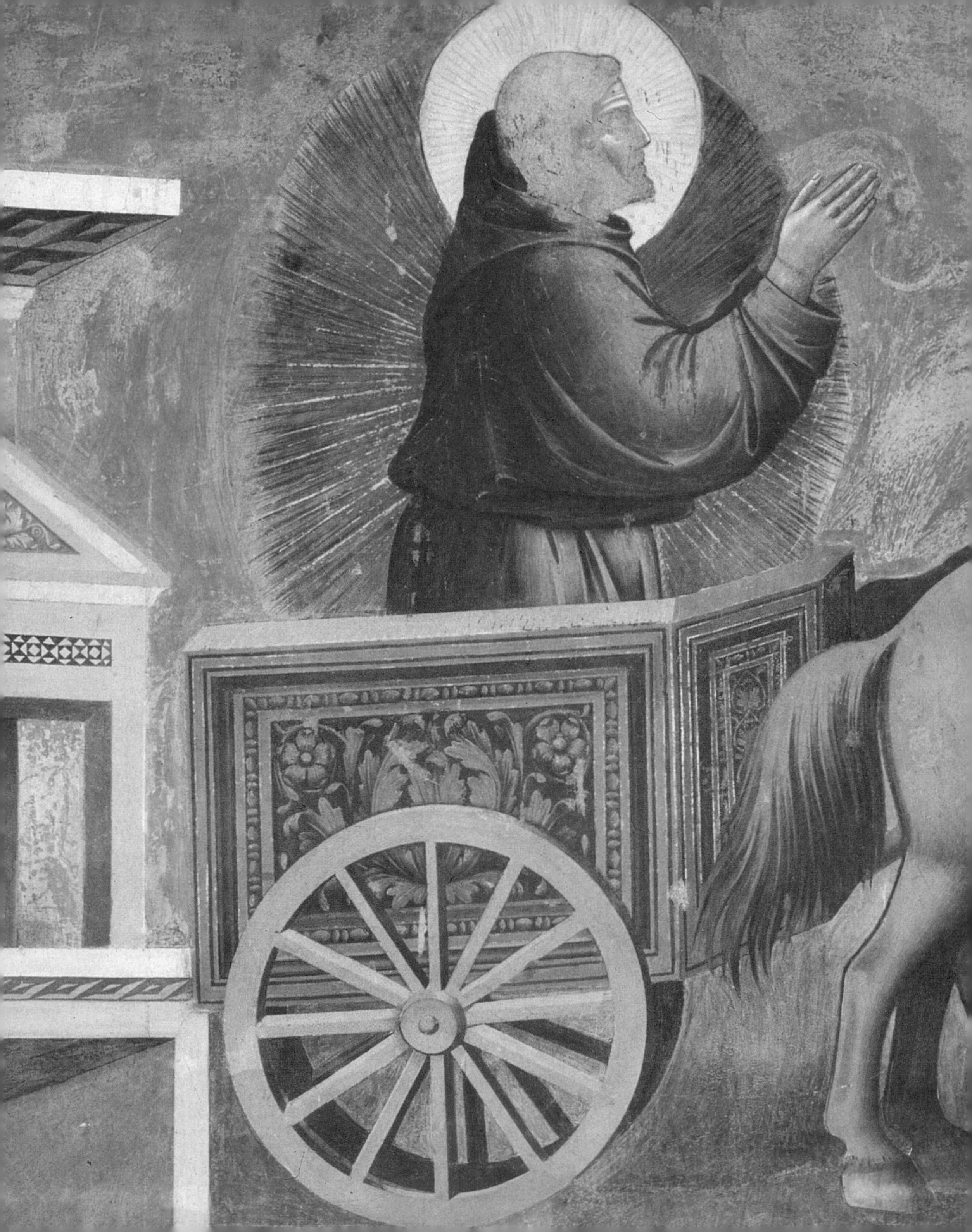

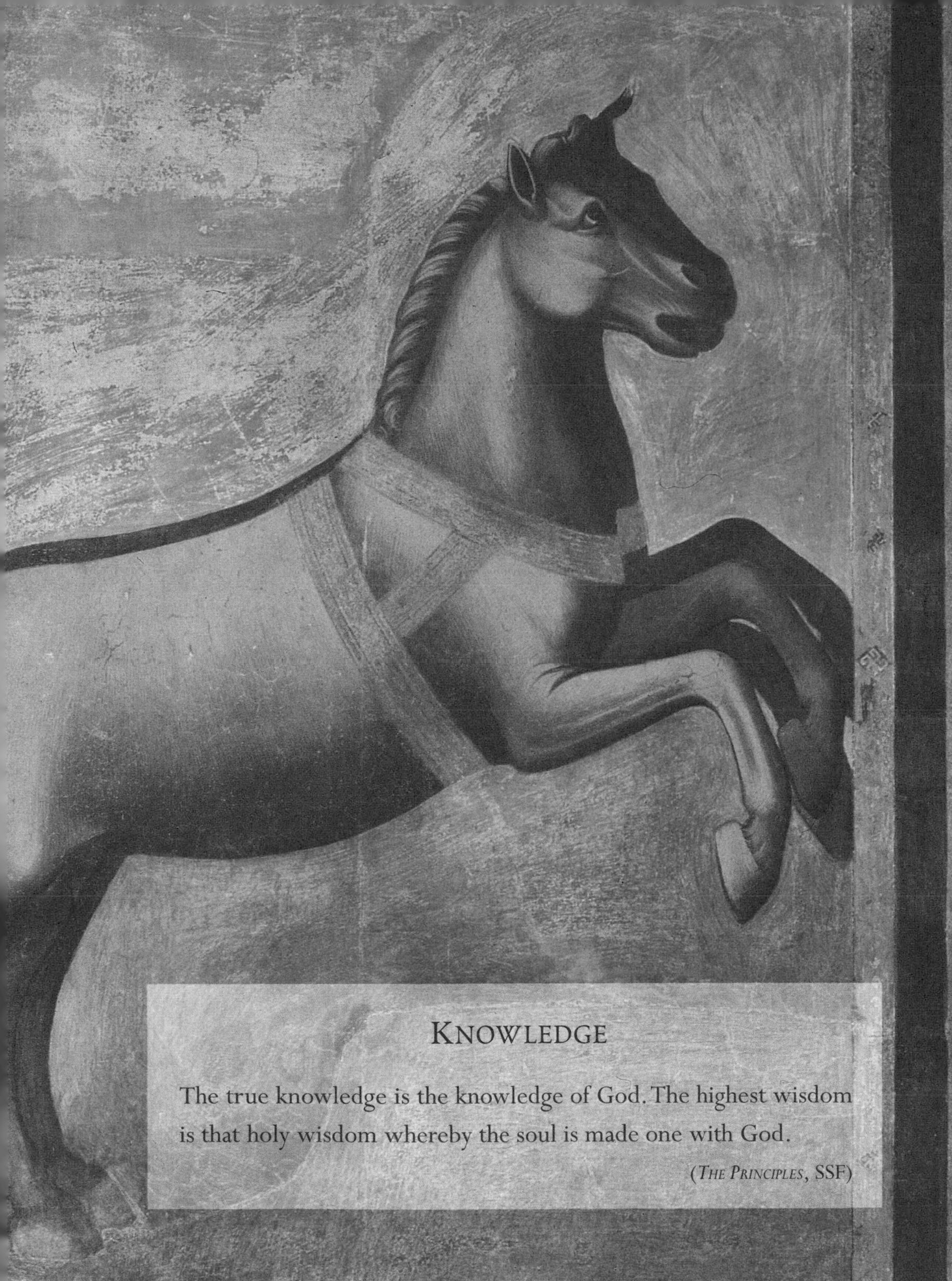

Knowledge

The true knowledge is the knowledge of God. The highest wisdom is that holy wisdom whereby the soul is made one with God.

(*The Principles*, SSF)

FRANCIS' COMPASSION FOR THE SICK

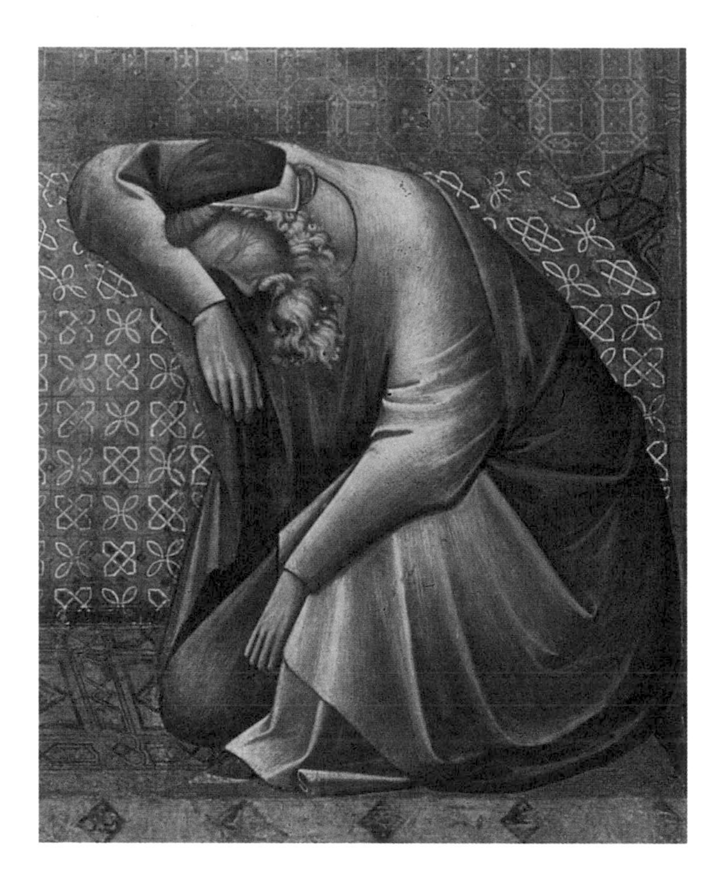

Francis once took a certain sick brother, who he knew had a longing for grapes, into the vineyard and sitting down under the vine, he first ate to give the other courage to eat.

(THOMAS OF CELANO, *THE SECOND LIFE OF ST FRANCIS,* CH. CXXXIII, NO. 176)

FRANCIS' DEVOTION TO THE ANGELS

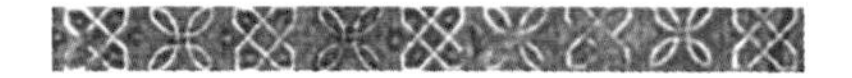

Francis venerated with a very great affection the angels who are with us in our struggle and who walk *in the midst of the shadow of death* with us. Such companions who were everywhere with us, he used to say, are to be venerated, such are to be invoked as our guardians. He used to teach that their presence must not be offended, and that we must not presume to do before them what we would not do before people.

(THOMAS OF CELANO, *THE SECOND LIFE OF ST FRANCIS,* CH. CXLIX, NO. 197)

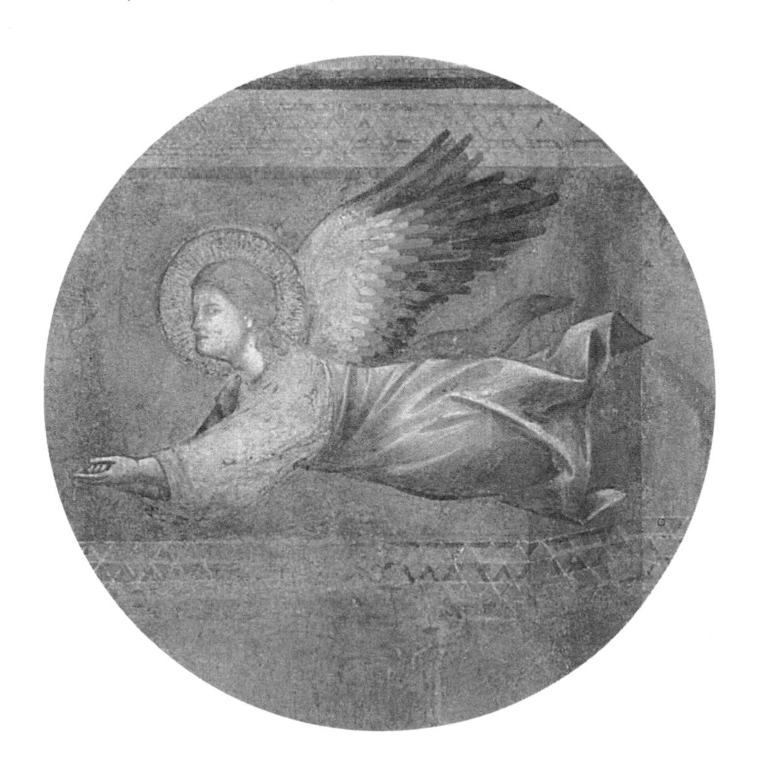

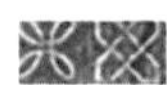

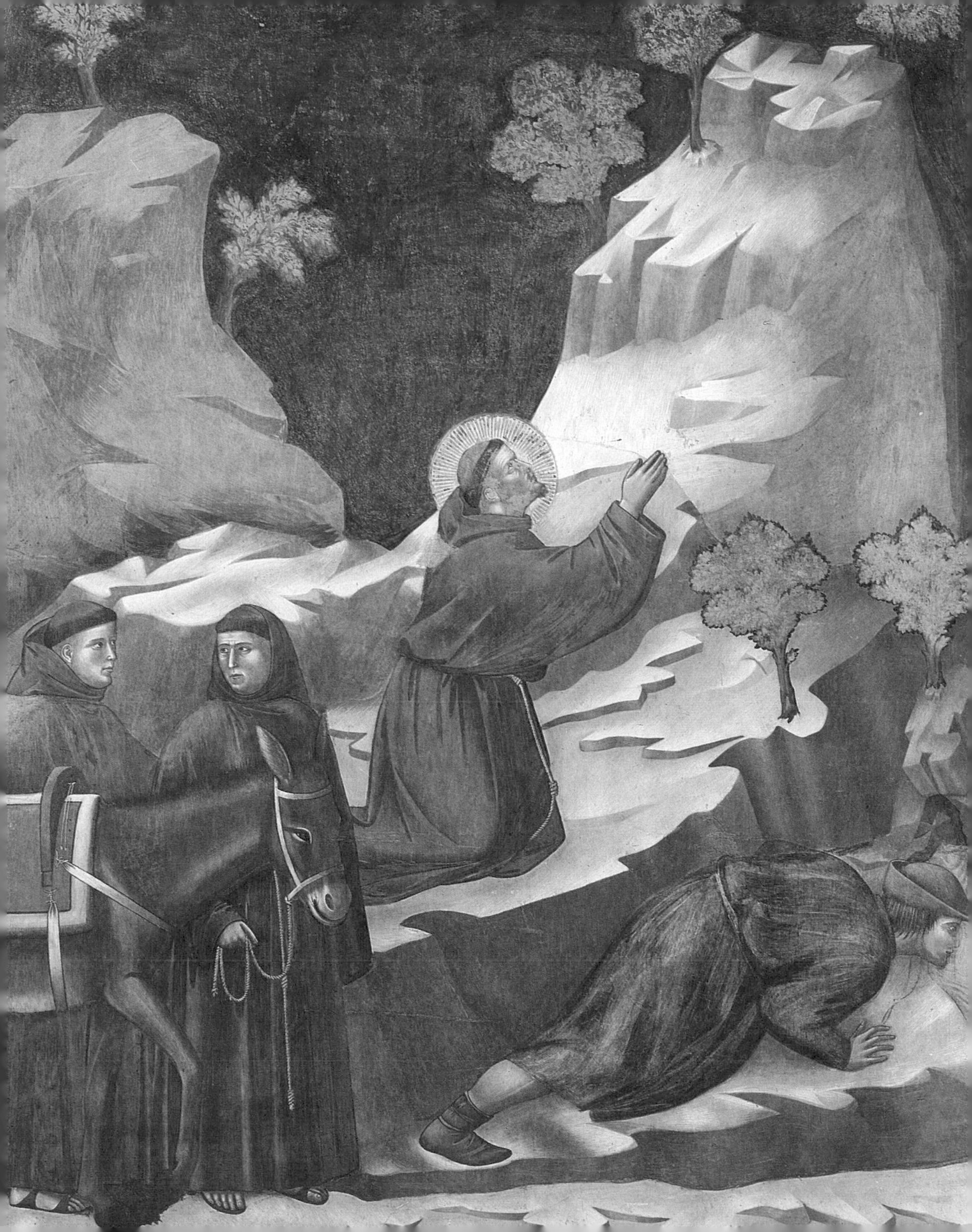

Francis Prays for a Miracle

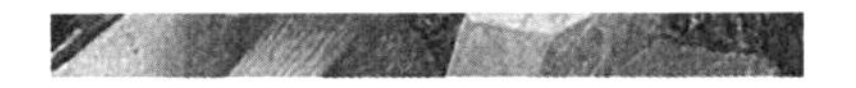

Once when the blessed Francis wanted to go to a certain hermitage that he might devote himself more freely to contemplation there, he obtained an ass from a certain poor man to ride on, because he was not a little weak. Since it was summer, the peasant, following the man of God up the mountain, became fatigued from the difficulty and the length of the trip; and before they had reached the place, he collapsed exhausted by a burning thirst. He called after the saint and begged him to have pity on him; he said he would die unless he would be refreshed by some drink. The holy man of God, who always had compassion on those who were suffering, got down without delay from the ass and kneeling upon the ground, he stretched his hands toward heaven; and he did not let up in his prayers until he felt he had been heard. "Hurry," he said to the peasant, "and you will find living water over there, which Christ has just now mercifully brought from the rock for you to drink."

(Thomas of Celano, *The Second Life of St Francis*, Ch. XVII, No. 46)

Purity of Heart

Blessed are the clean of heart, for they shall see God. A man is really clean of heart when he has no time for the things of this world but is always searching for the things of heaven, never failing to keep God before his eyes and always adoring him with a pure heart and soul.

(*The Admonitions*, XVI)

The Humble Religious

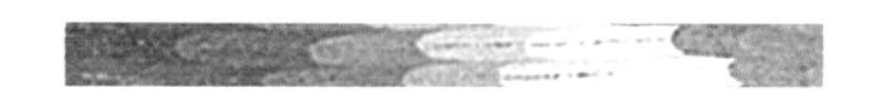

Blessed the religious who takes no more pride in the good that God says and does through him, than in that which he says and does through someone else. It is wrong for anyone to be anxious to receive more from his neighbour than he himself is willing to give to God.

(*The Admonitions*, XVII)

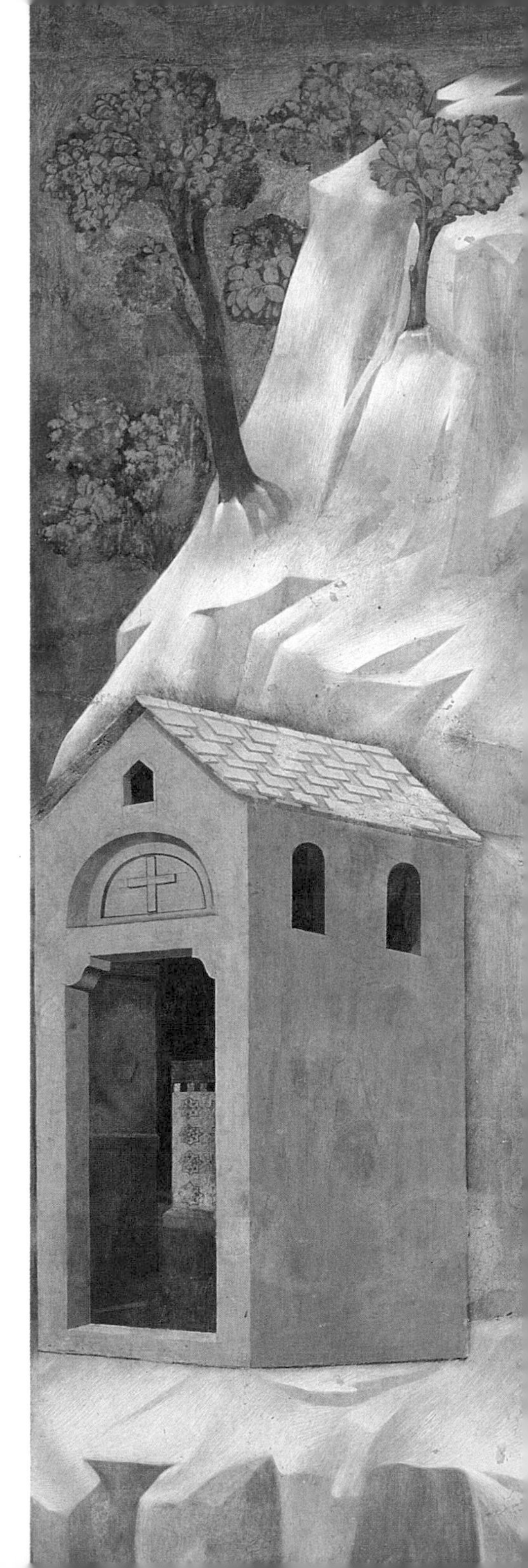

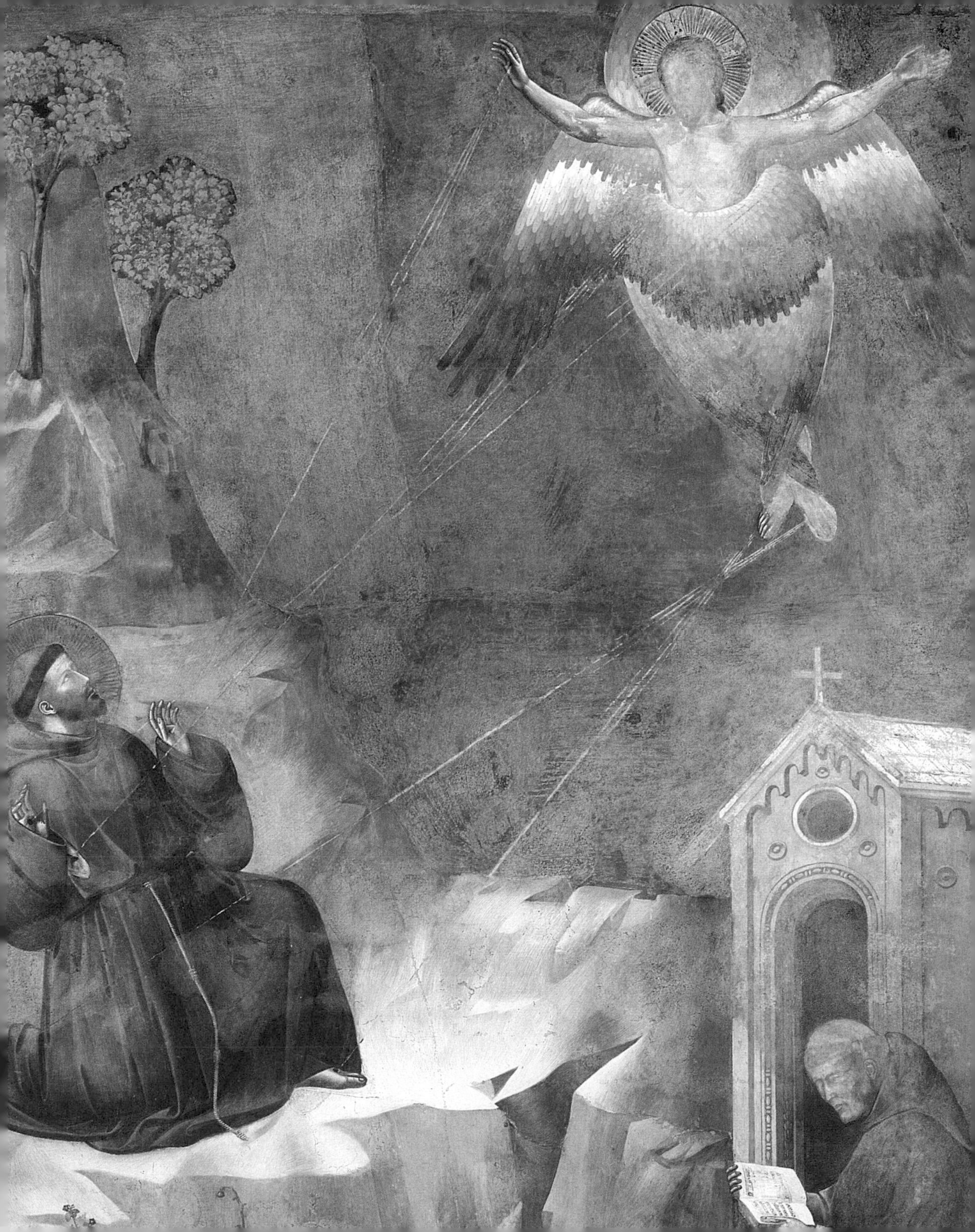

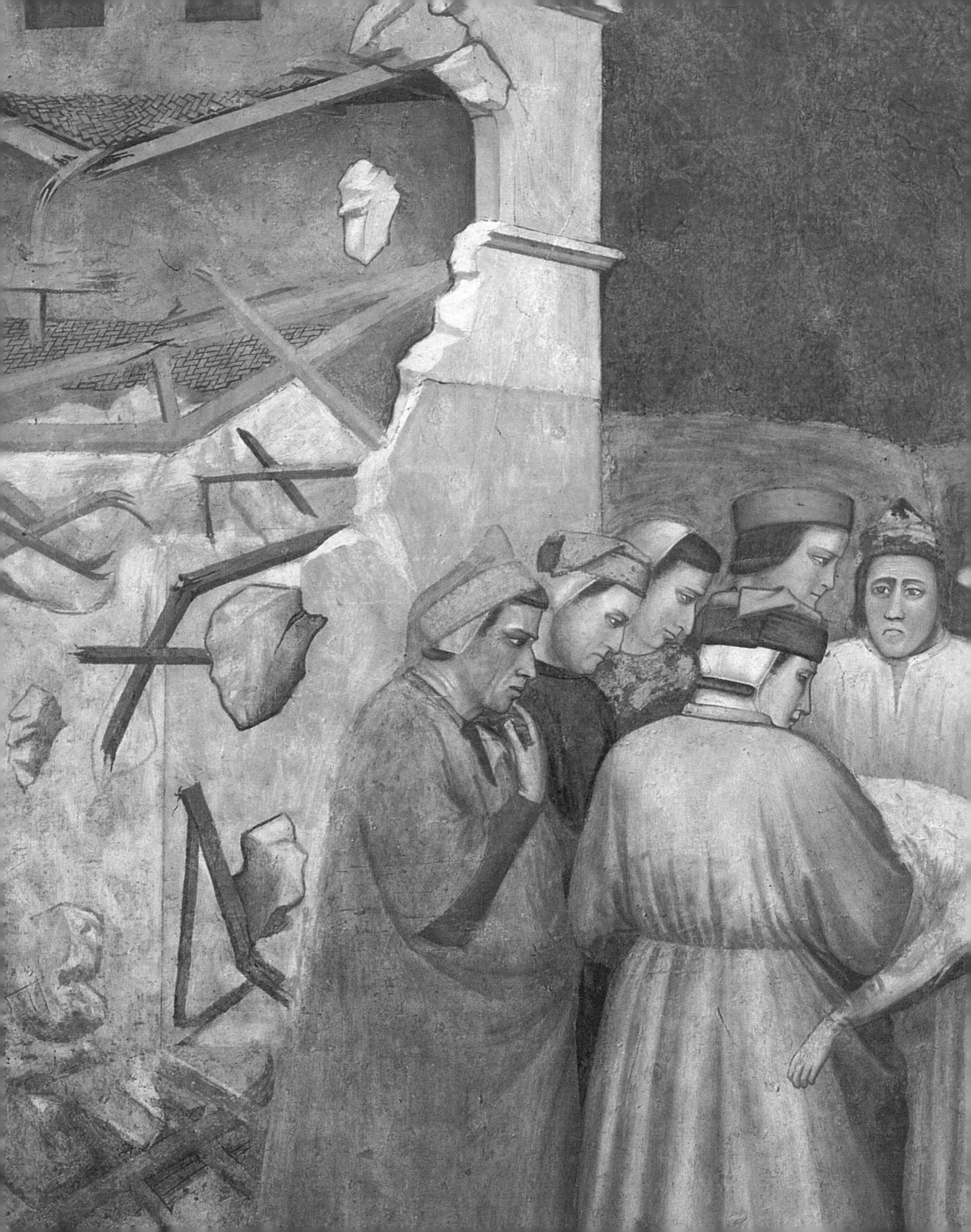

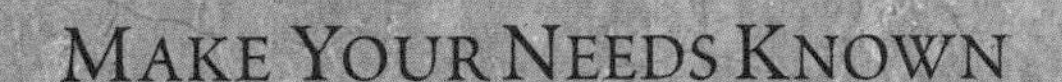

Make Your Needs Known

The friars should have no hesitation about telling one another what they need, so that they can provide for one another. They are bound to love and care for one another as brothers, according to the means God gives them, just as a mother loves and cares for her son.

(*Rule of 1221*, Ch. IX)

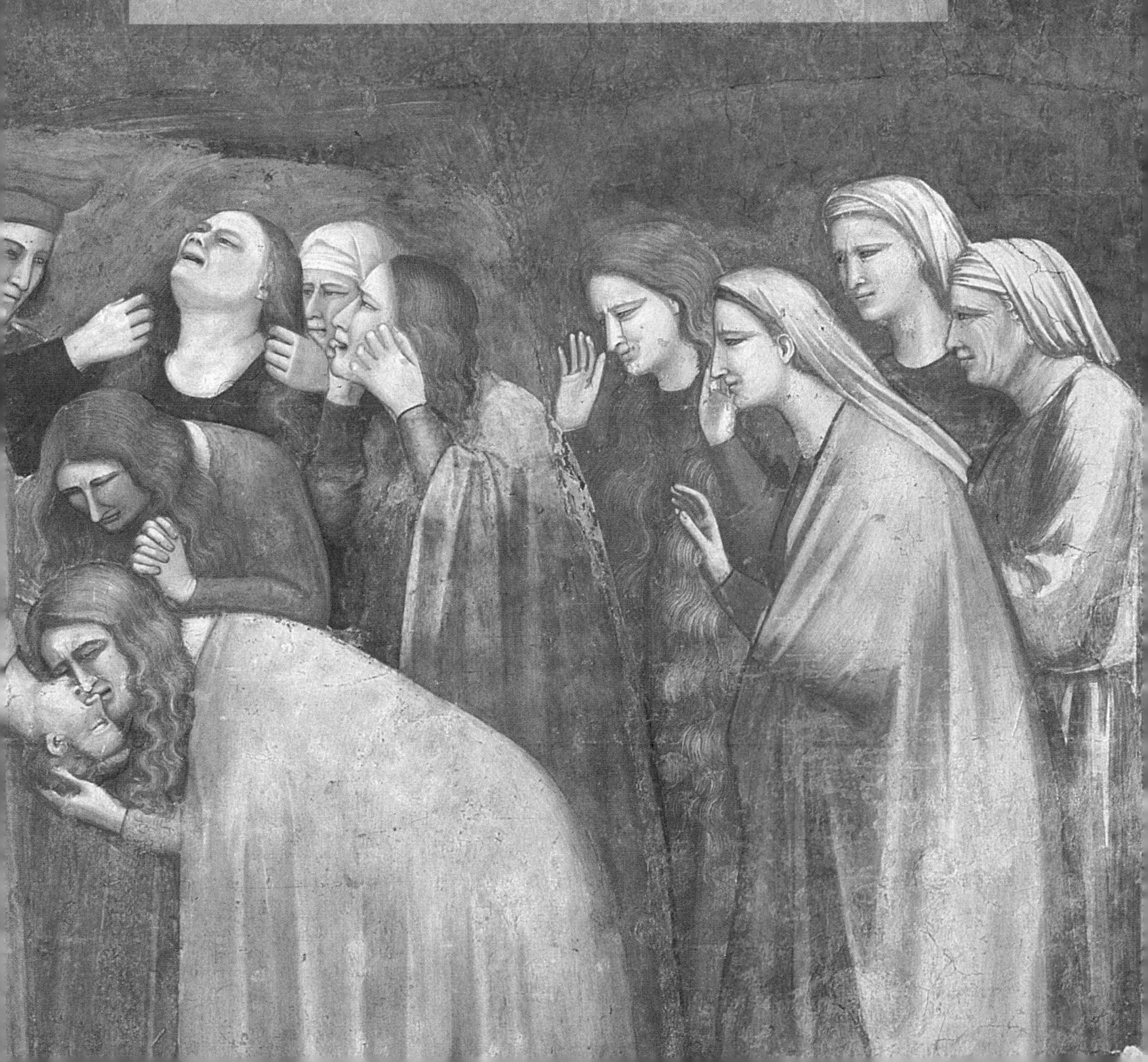

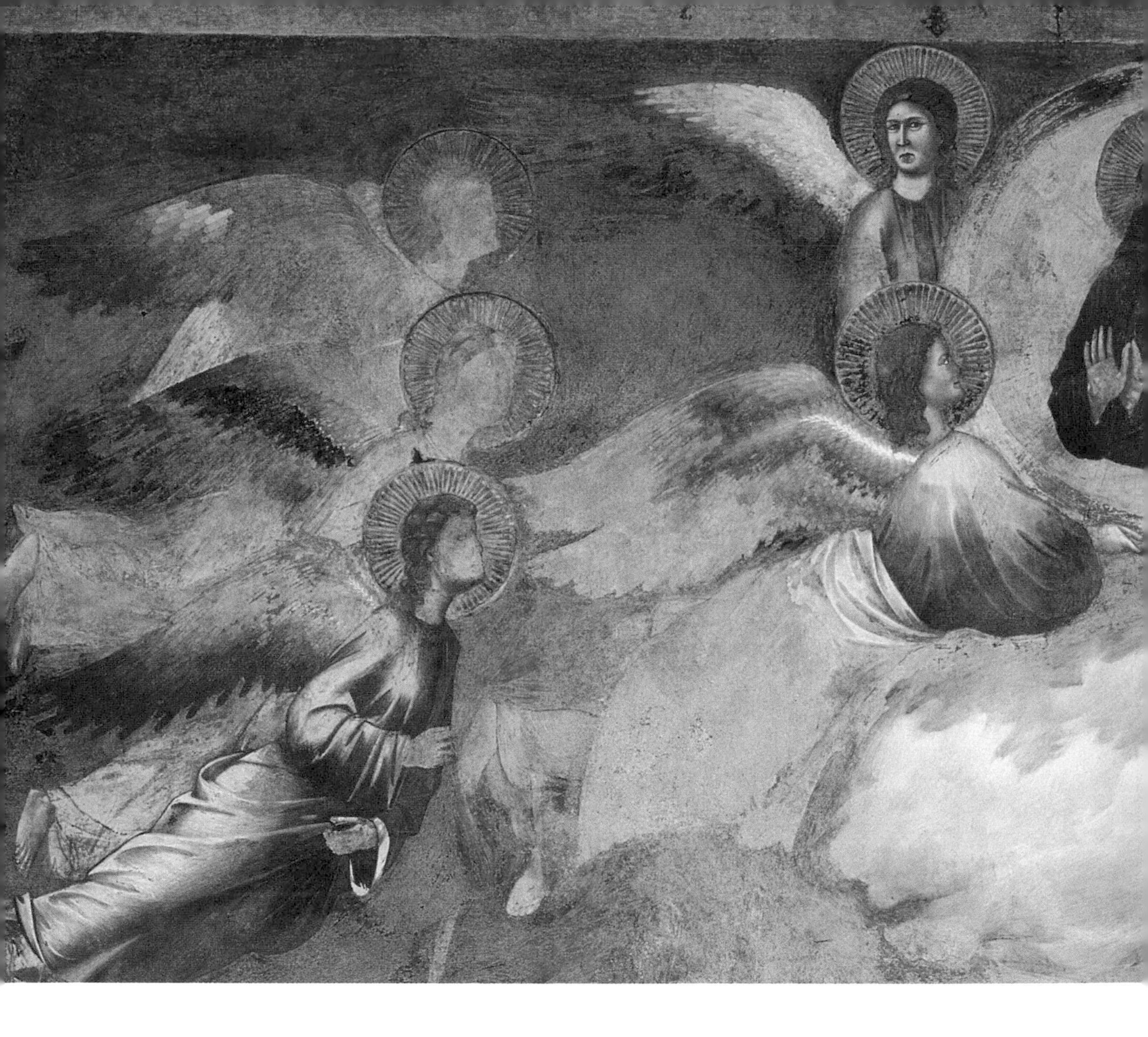

A Star Amid the Clouds

By the glorious splendour of his life and teaching Francis shone like the day-star amid the clouds, and by the brilliance which radiated from him he guided those who live in darkness, in the shadow of death, to the light.

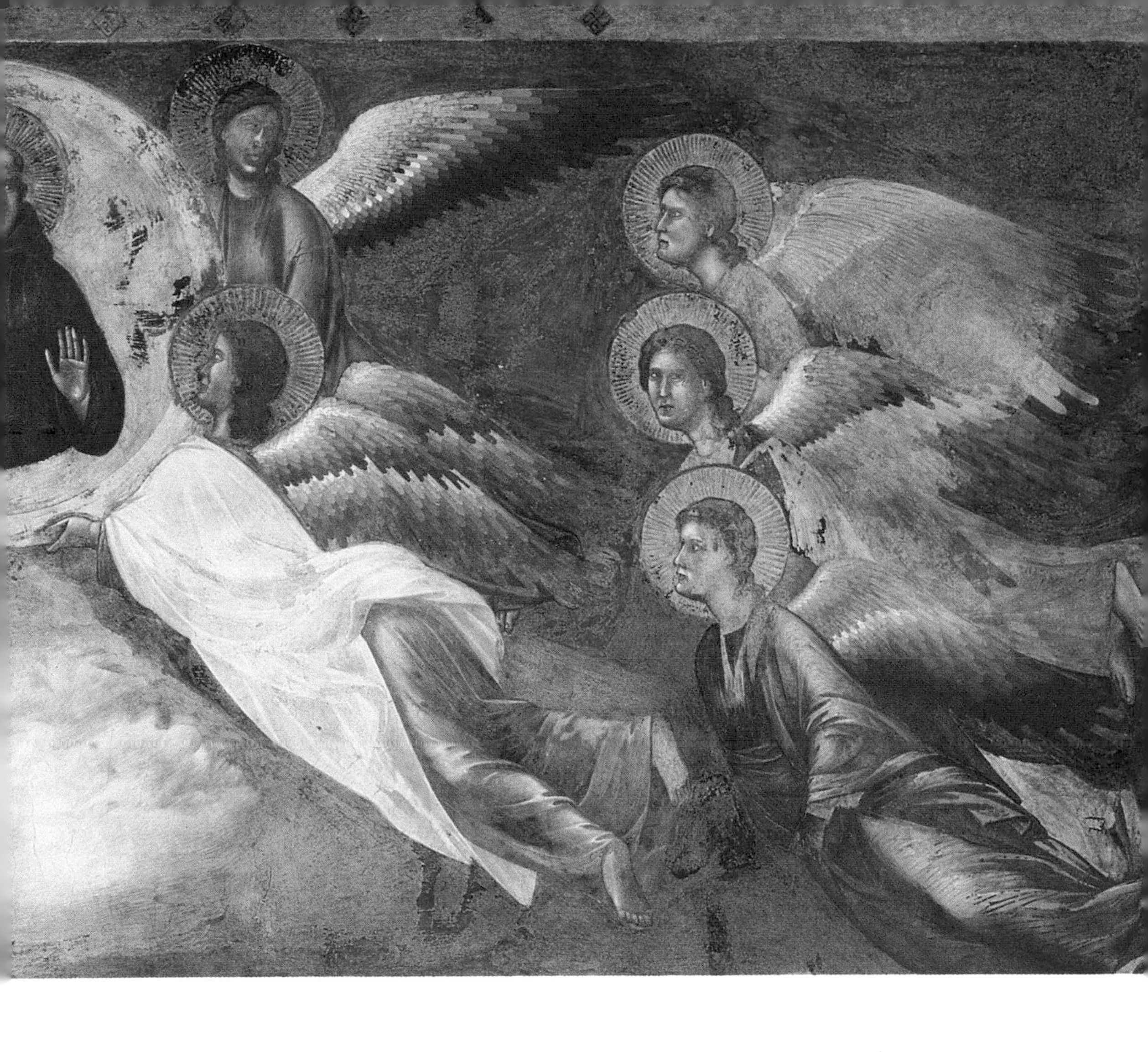

Like the rainbow that lights up the clouds with sudden glory, he bore in his own body the pledge of God's covenant, bringing the good news of peace and salvation to men, like a true angel of peace.

(ST BONAVENTURE, *MAJOR LIFE OF ST FRANCIS*, PREFACE, NO. 1)

Index of Frescoes

The frescoes in the Upper Church at Assisi showing the life of St Francis were probably painted in the 1290s. Scholars have argued for years over who the artists were. We do not know whether Giotto was one of them, or even their supervisor; all we know from early sources is that he was there, and the clarity and simplicity of the frescoes is similar in style to his work. For the medieval viewer such questions were immaterial - it would have been the message, not the messenger, that counted.

The 28 scenes from the saint's life encircle the nave walls of the Upper Church, beginning and ending at the crossing, below the biblical scenes. The episodes shown are from *Major Life of St Francis*, the authorised biography of the saint written around 1263 by St Bonaventure. They were painted in a way that made the stories intelligible to the least-informed viewer and chosen specifically for their symbolic links with the biblical scenes above.

The first four scenes cover the saint's life as a young man. The cycle opens with *Francis honoured by a Simple Man*, when a "holy fool" recognises the saintliness of Francis. Medieval viewers would have recognised this scene as a reference to the entry of Christ in Jerusalem before his Passion. In scene II, Francis performs his first act of charity: he gives away his cloak to the poor knight, a reminder to members of the congregation that they too should practice charity. In *The Prayer in front of the Cross in San Damiano* (IV) and *The Dream of Innocent III* (VI), Francis is revealed as restorer and upholder of the church, in both a physical and a spiritual sense.

All the frescoes emphasise Francis' humility: in *The Confirmation of the Rule* (VII), Francis and his companions kneel meekly before the Pope and curia, although it is they who are in need of the Franciscans' spirituality. The reward for the saint's humility is the riches he will receive in heaven, often revealed in dreams and visions, as in *The Vision of the Palace* (III) or *The Vision of the Thrones* (IX). In the latter, Francis kneels in prayer before the altar while Brother Pacificus sees the angels' thrones. The most splendid throne – which, according to St Bonaventure, belonged to a fallen angel – will be for Francis himself.

The scenes around the entrance (X - XIX) show the saint preaching and performing miracles. There are parallels here with the life of Christ, particularly in *Francis receiving the Stigmata*, where Christ himself appears, embraced by seraphim. The remaining scenes depict Francis' death, funeral and posthumous miracles. *The Death of Francis* (XX) shows him rising towards heaven, echoing Christ's Ascension after the Resurrection, and the Assumption of the Virgin Mary. *Clare mourning Francis' Body* (XXIII) recalls the Lamentation, another event in the life of Mary.

During lengthy sermons, the congregation had plenty of time to absorb the messages of peace, humility and joy which the images convey. As they left the Church, their last view would have been two of the most famous Franciscan stories, *The Preaching to the Birds* and *The Miracle of the Spring*, immediately below the New Testament scenes of Pentecost and the Ascension. Perhaps it was these images of hope which lingered on in their hearts and minds.

Plan of the Basilica

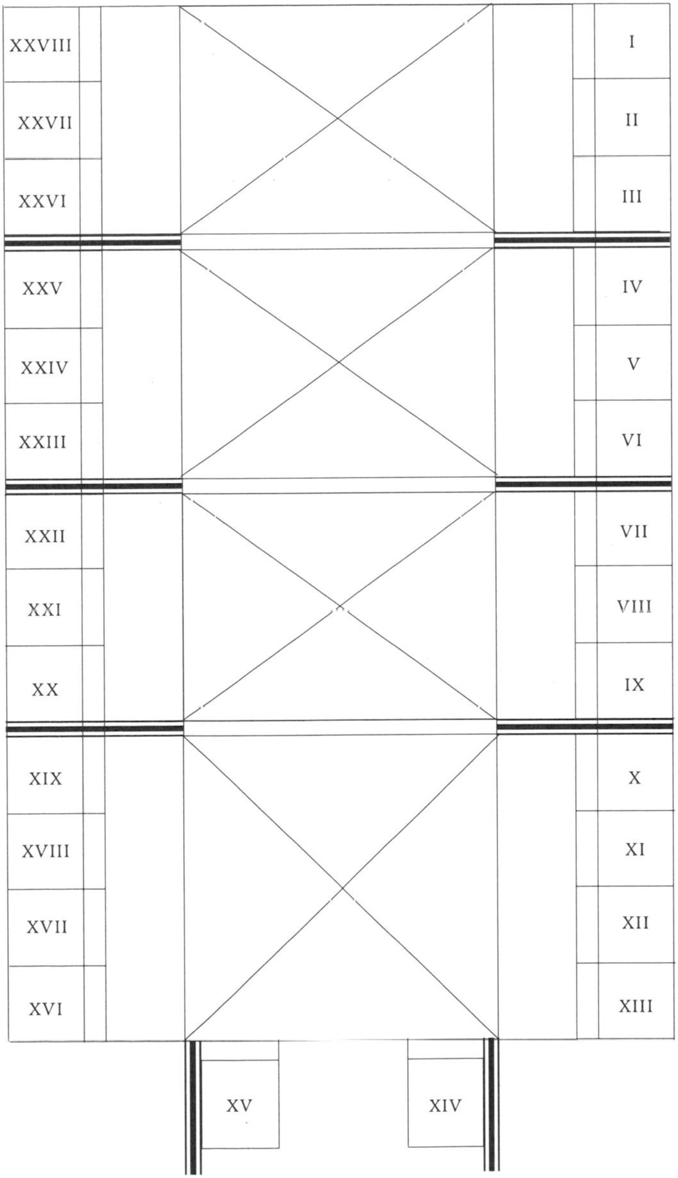

XXVIII
XXVII
XXVI
XXV
XXIV
XXIII
XXII
XXI
XX
XIX
XVIII
XVII
XVI

I
II
III
IV
V
VI
VII
VIII
IX
X
XI
XII
XIII

XV
XIV

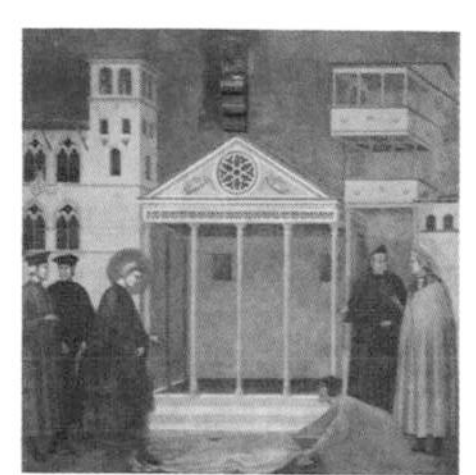

I Francis honoured by a Simple Man
pages 8-9

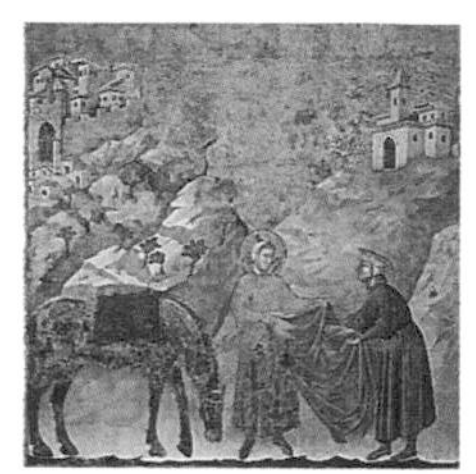

II Francis giving his Mantle to a Poor Knight
cover & pages 28, 32-33

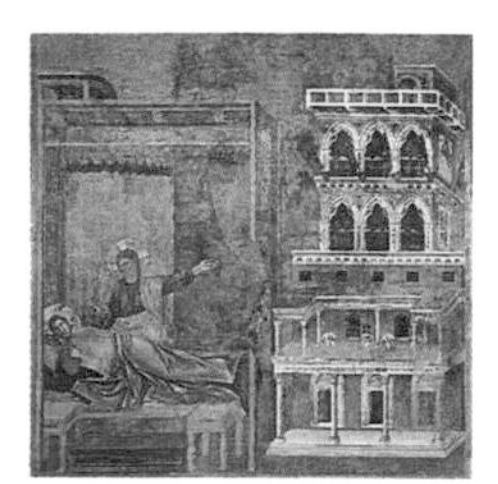

III The Vision of the Palace
page 36

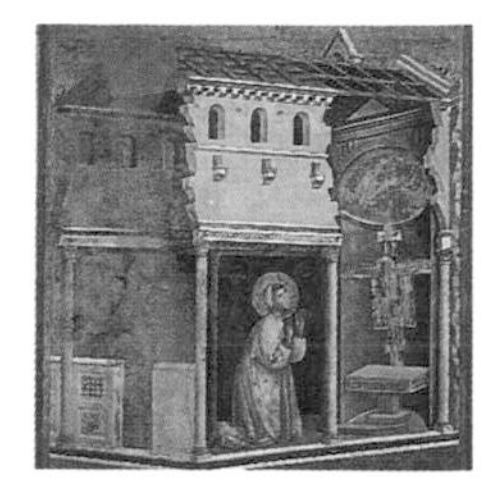

IV The Prayer in front of the Cross in San Damiano
page 6

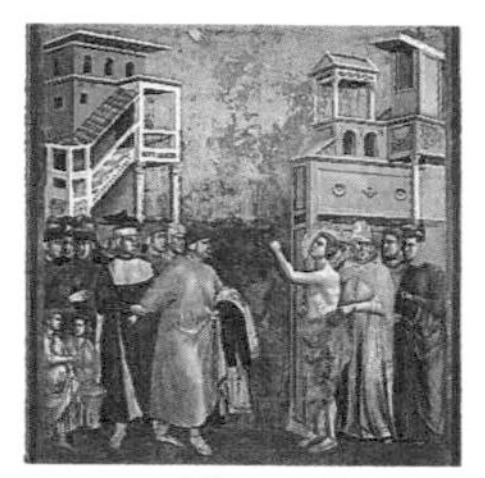

V Francis' Renunciation of his Father's Inheritance
page 44

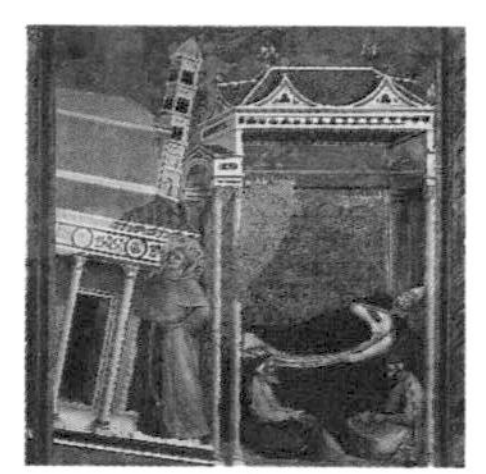

VI The Dream of Innocent III
pages 10-11

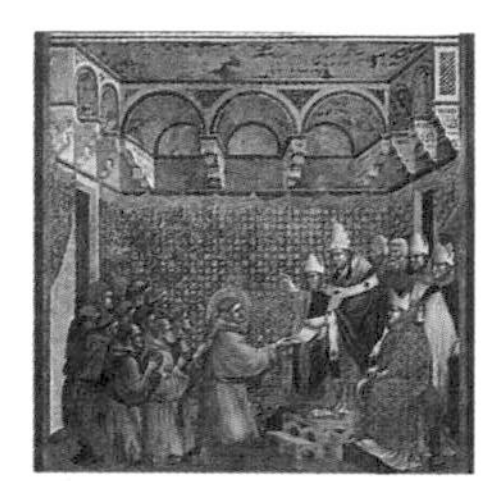

VII The Confirmation of the Rule
pages 2-3, 12-13, 62-63

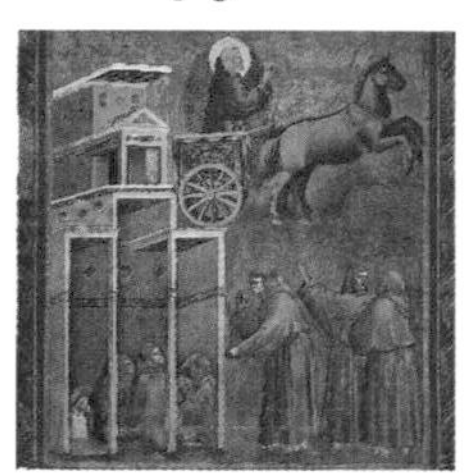

VIII The Vision of Francis borne on a Fiery Chariot
pages 46-47

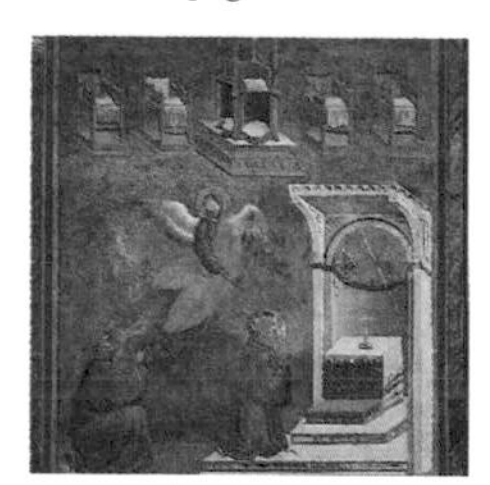

IX The Vision of the Thrones
page 17

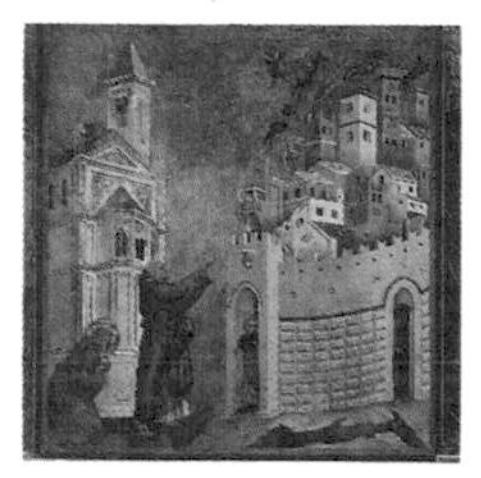

X The Expulsion of the Devils from the City of Arezzo
pages 20, 37

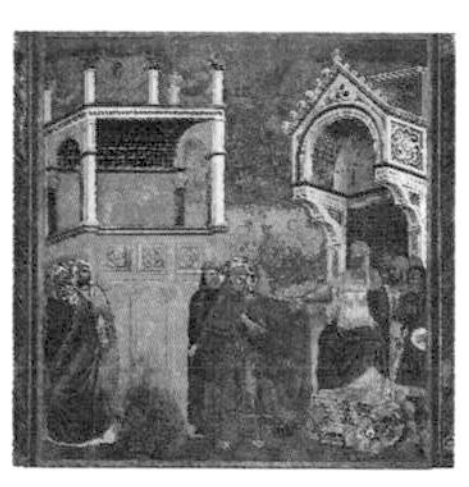

XI The Ordeal by Fire before the Sultan
page 29

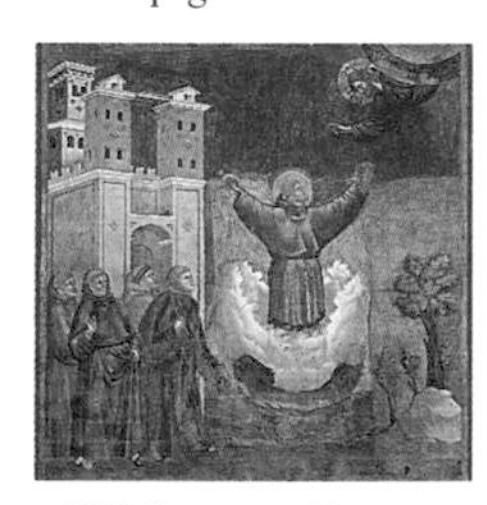

XII Francis in Ecstasy
pages 38-39

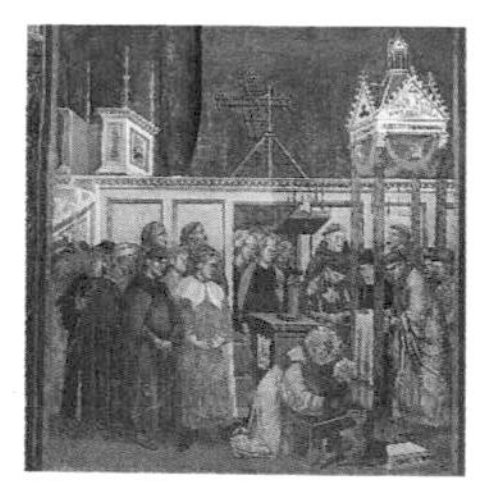

XIII The Crib at Greccio
pages 42-43

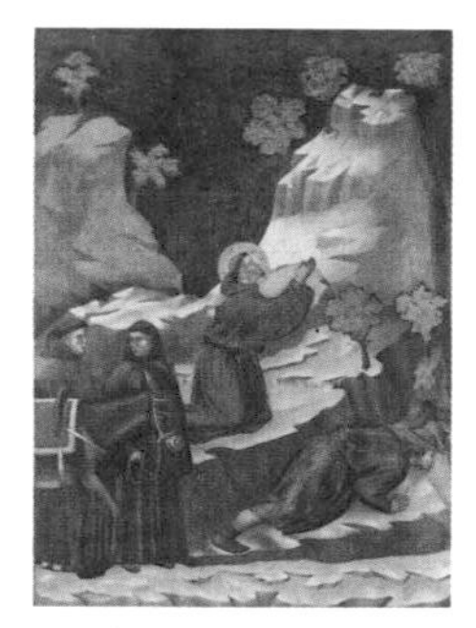

XIV The Miracle of the Water that gushed from the Rock
pages 50-51

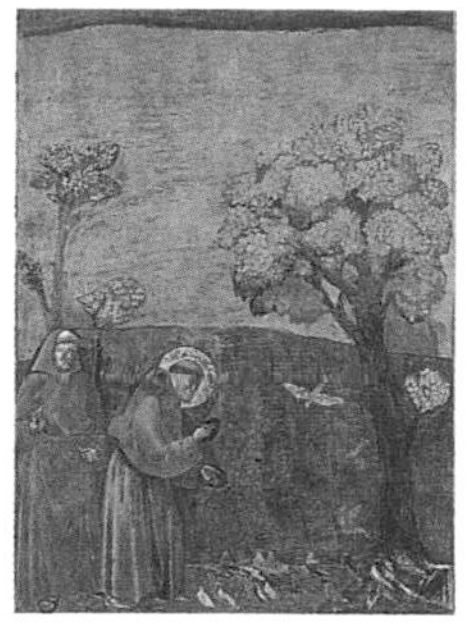

XV The Preaching to the Birds
pages 30-31

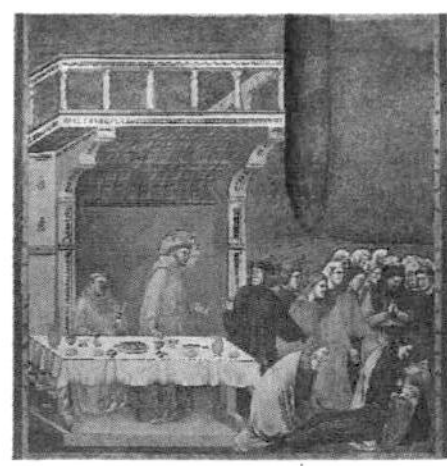

XVI The Death of the Knight of Celano
pages 18, 34-35

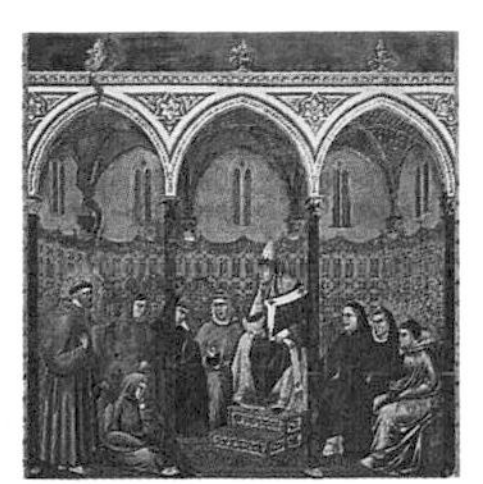

XVII Francis preaching before Honorius III
PAGES 14-15

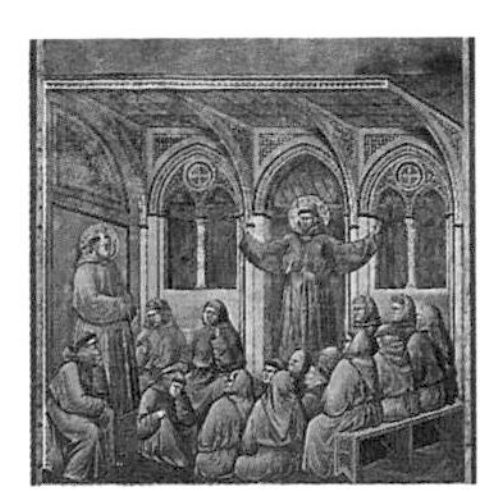

XVIII The Apparition at Arles

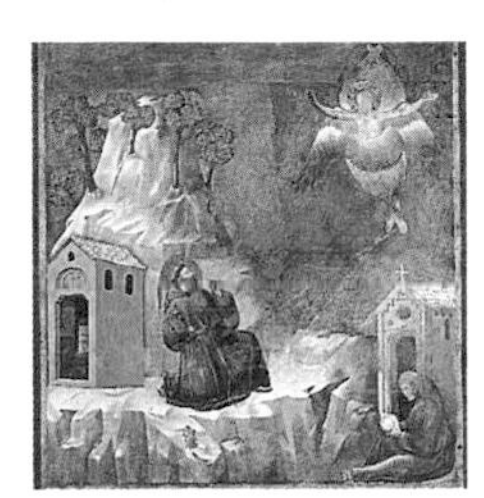

XIX Francis receiving the Stigmata
PAGES 52-53

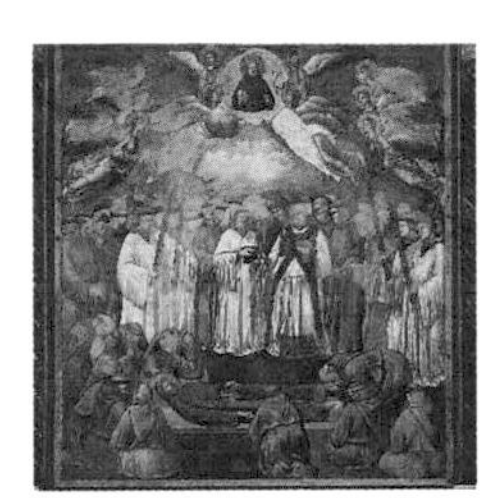

XX The Death of Francis
PAGES 56-57

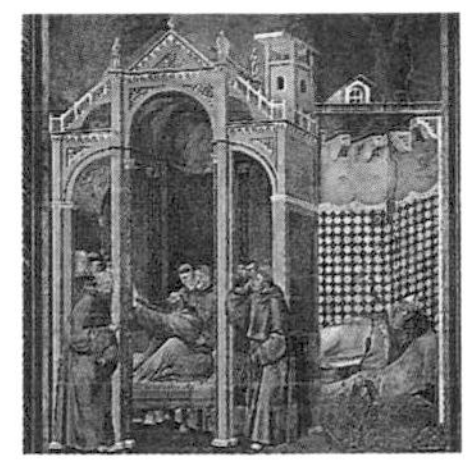

XXI The Vision of Brother Augustine and the Bishop of Assisi
PAGE 19

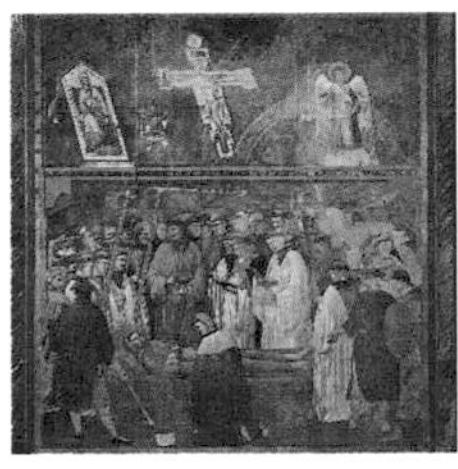

XXII The Verification of the Stigmata

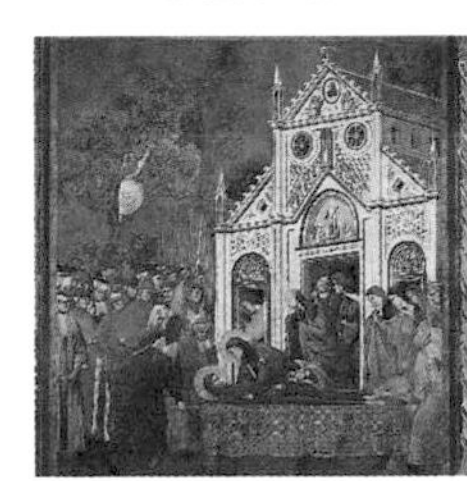

XXIII Clare mourning Francis' Body
PAGES 26, 45

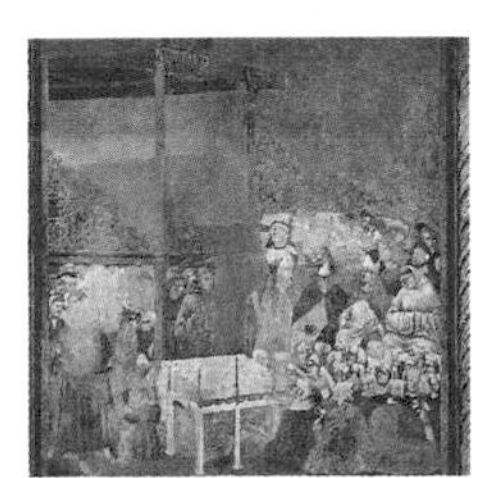

XXIV The Canonization of Francis
PAGES 22-23

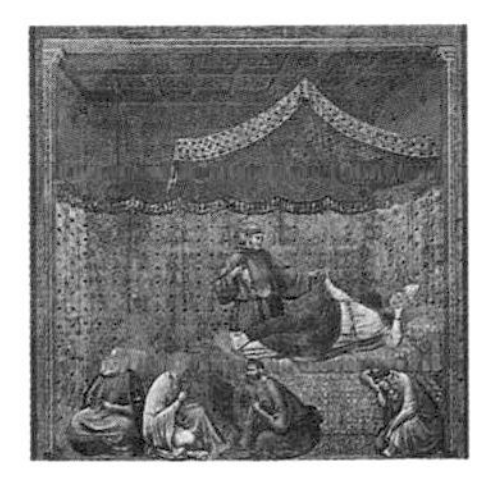

XXV The Appearance to Gregory IX
PAGES 5, 48

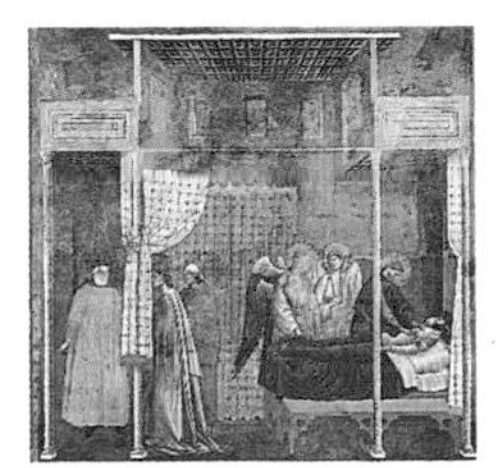

XXVI The Healing of a Knight of Ilerda
PAGE 16

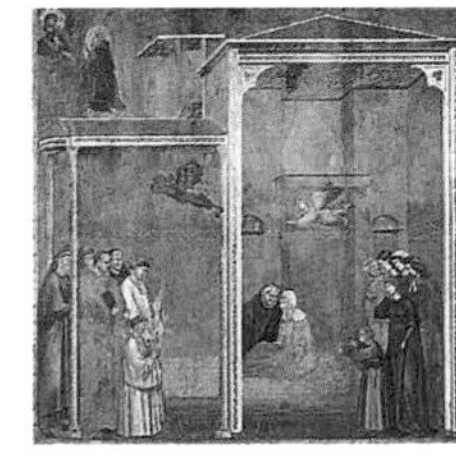

XXVII The Confession of a Woman raised from the Dead
PAGES 26,27,49

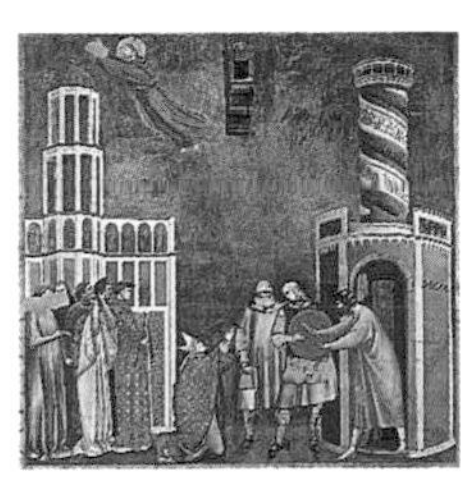

XXVIII The Liberation of the Repentant Heretic
PAGES 40-41

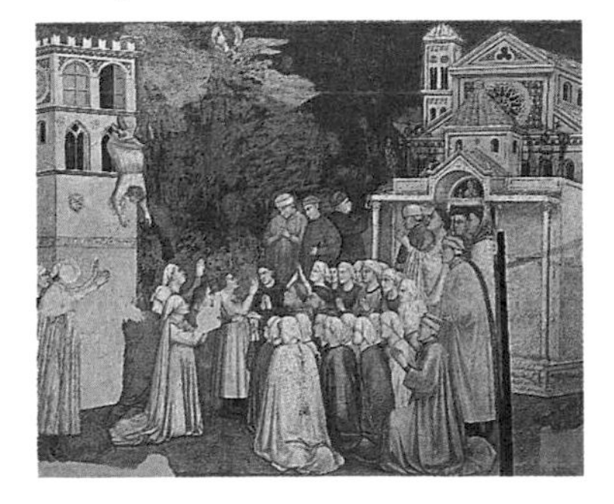

The Raising of the Boy who fell from the Balcony
PAGES 24-25

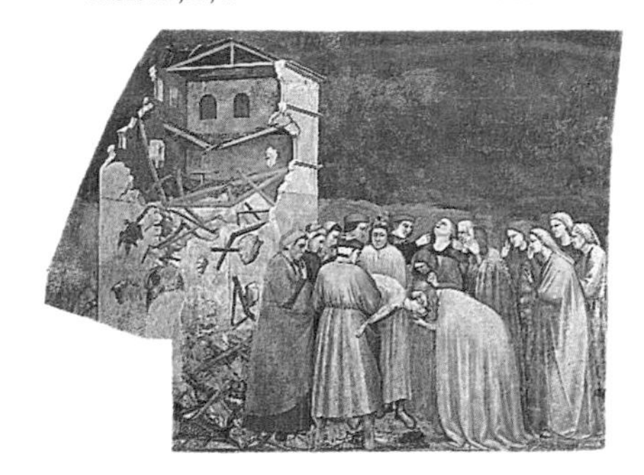

The Death of the Boy in Sessa
PAGES 54-55

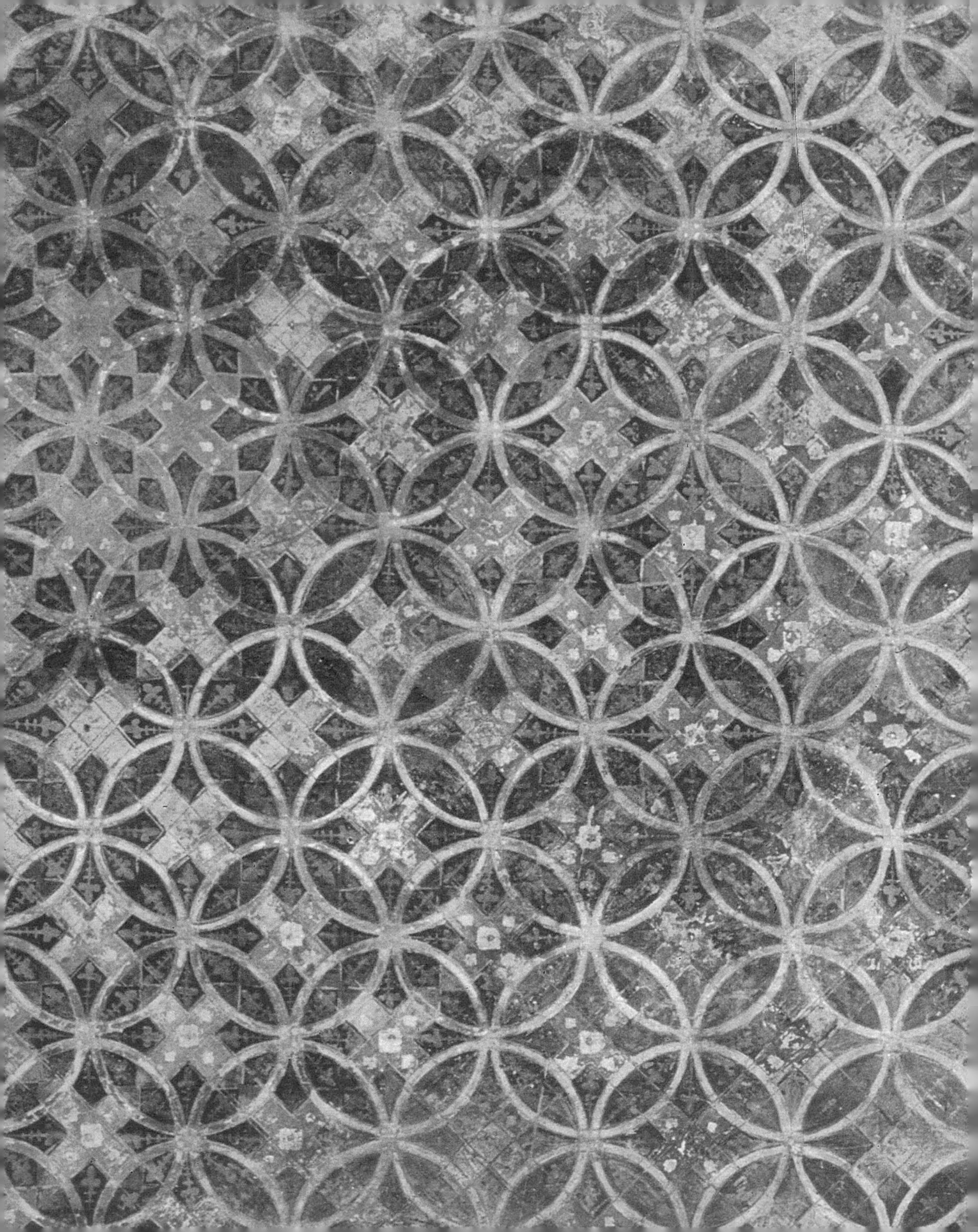